Urbanizing the Mojave Desert: Las Vegas
Die Urbanisierung der Mojave-Wüste: Las Vegas

jovis

Urbanizing the Mojave Desert: Las Vegas
Die Urbanisierung der Mojave-Wüste: Las Vegas

Text and Photographs by Nicole Huber and Ralph Stern
Text und Fotografien von Nicole Huber und Ralph Stern

jovis

© 2008 by jovis Verlag GmbH
Das Copyright für die Texte liegt bei den Autoren.
Das Copyright für die Abbildungen liegt bei den Fotografen/Inhabern der Bildrechte.
Texts by kind permission of the authors.
Pictures by kind permission of the photographers/holders of the picture rights.

Übersetzung I Translation: Nicole Huber
Gestaltung und Satz I Design and Setting: CURNetwork
Lithografie I Lithography: Bild1Druck, Berlin
Druck und Bindung I Printing and Binding: OAN Offizin Andersen Nexö Leipzig, Zwenkau

Bibliografische Information der Deutschen Bibliothek
Die Deutsche Bibliothek verzeichnet diese Publikation in der Deutschen Nationalbibliografie; detail-
lierte bibliografische Daten sind im Internet über http://dnb.ddb.de abrufbar.
Bibliographic information published by Die Deutsche Bibliothek
Die Deutsche Bibliothek lists this publication in the Deutsche Nationalbibliografie; detailed bibliographic
data are available in the Internet at http://dnb.ddb.de

jovis Verlag
Kurfürstenstraße 15/16
10785 Berlin

www.jovis.de

ISBN 978-3-939633-50-1

Danksagung

Das Engagement vieler Menschen hat *Die Urbanisierung der Mojave-Wüste: Las Vegas* möglich gemacht, denen wir an dieser Stelle für ihre Unterstützung und Ermutigung danken wollen. Daniel Friedman, Dave Miller und Vikram Prakash vom College of Architecture and Urban Planning der University of Washington förderten die Realisierung des Projekts äußerst großzügig. Außerdem erhielt das Buch durch das Johnston/Hastings Publication Support Endowment bedeutende Unterstützung. Als kooperierender Partner spielte das von Nancy Levinson geleitete Phoenix Urban Research Laboratory (PURL, College of Design, Arizona State University) eine zentrale Rolle. Das Symposium *Sites of Transition: Urbanizing the Mojave Desert*, das PURL zusammen mit ASU Future Arts Research und ASUs School of Art und dessen Art Museum organisierte, wie auch die Diskussionen mit Lucy Lippard, Mark Klett, Matt Coolidge und Bruce Ferguson, waren für die Fertigstellung unseres Projekts sehr förderlich. Die Vorschläge von Michael Dear, Vikram Prakash, Peter Carl, Ron Smith und David Wrobel zum Text waren sehr kenntnisreich und konstruktiv. Die Cultural Section der United States Embassy in Berlin und das Team vom Deutschen Architektur Zentrum Berlin (DAZ) halfen beide, das Projekt einem internationalen Publikum zugänglich zu machen. Jochen Visscher und sein Team vom JOVIS Verlag waren mit ihrer Hilfe und Geduld außergewöhnlich.

In Nevada erhielt das Buch Unterstützung vom Nevada Arts Council. Joan Lolmaugh und Mark Hall-Patton von Clark County Parks and Recreation begrüßten die Dokumentation von Veränderungen ihrer geliebten Region enthusiastisch. An der University of Nevada Las Vegas zeigte sich Paul Aizley wahrhaft vorbildlich in seinen Bemühungen, eine raue Umgebung zu humanisieren. Unser besonderer Dank gilt auch den Studierenden von UNLV's School of Architecture, besonders Lina Mehyar, Chris Lujan, Dan Brown und Tommy Huggins standen diesem Projekt mit Rat und Tat zur Seite. In gleicher Weise waren die Studierenden des Las Vegas design studio der University of Washington einsichtige Kritiker vorherrschender Urbanisierungstendenzen.

Viele andere könnten erwähnt werden, unerlässlich ist es, das Augenmerk auf Elizabeth Gray Kogen zu richten, die allerorts auf indianische Kultur achtete, das Kleingedruckte auf Geschichtstafeln sorgsam las und die endlosen Stopps zum Fotografieren geduldig ertrug. Dazu kommt Sabine Cofalla, eine Literaturwissenschaftlerin und leidenschaftliche Wanderin, die turbulente Tage erlebte, als wir auf Seitenstraßen gemeinsam durch den Schneesturm über das Colorado Plateau fuhren. Und schließlich gilt Andrea Huber unser größter Dank. Sie unterstützte uns rückhaltlos und hielt die Stellung, wenn wir uns in die städtischen Grenzgebiete aufmachten.

Acknowledgements

Urbanizing the Mojave Desert: Las Vegas has crossed the paths of many individuals deserving recognition for their support and encouragement. Daniel Friedman, Dave Miller and Vikram Prakash of the College of Architecture and Urban Planning at the University of Washington have been extremely gracious and generous in their assistance. This book also received substantial support through the Johnston/Hastings Publication Support Endowment. As a cooperating partner, the Phoenix Urban Research Laboratory (PURL, College of Design, Arizona State University) directed by Nancy Levinson was central in moving this project towards a successful conclusion. The *Sites of Transition: Urbanizing the Mojave Desert* symposium organized by PURL together with ASU Future Arts Research as well as ASU's School of Art and Art Museum was instrumental in finalizing our project ideas, as were conversations with Lucy Lippard, Mark Klett, Matt Coolidge, and Bruce Ferguson. The suggestions of Michael Dear, Vikram Prakash, Peter Carl, Ron Smith, and David Wrobel regarding the text were very insightful and constructive. The Cultural Section of the United States Embassy Berlin and the personnel of the German Architecture Center (DAZ) Berlin were central in making the project available to an international public. Jochen Visscher and his staff at JOVIS Publishers have been exceptional in their assistance and patience.

In Nevada, the book received the support of the Nevada Arts Council. Joan Lolmaugh and Mark Hall-Patton with Clark County Parks and Recreation lent their enthusiastic support to documenting changes in a region they love. At the University of Nevada Las Vegas Paul Aizley provided exceptional support, serving as an exemplar in his efforts to humanize a harsh environment. Special thanks must also be extended to UNLV's students, who have been enthusiastic supporters of new approaches to old problems. In particular Lina Mehyar, Chris Lujan, Dan Brown and Tommy Huggins did much to assist this project in work and spirit. Similarly, students of the University of Washington's Las Vegas design studio were insightful critics of the prevalent modes of urban development.

Many others could be mentioned. One that must is Elizabeth Gray Kogen, attending to sites of Native American culture, carefully reading the fine print on historic markers, and patiently enduring endless stops for photography. Also Sabine Cofalla, a literary scholar and determined hiker who encountered stormy days whilst driving together on back roads as icy snows blew across the Colorado Plateau. Finally, Andrea Huber has been undivided in her support, holding down the fort while we set off across this urban frontier.

Orte des Übergangs:
Die Urbanisierung der Mojave-Wüste

Dieses Buch dokumentiert Urbanisierungsprozesse im Las Vegas Valley und der Mojave-Wüste jenseits der berühmten Spektakel des Las Vegas Strip. Als Metropolregion, die über zwei Millionen Einwohner umfasst, hat sich Las Vegas von einem Wüsten-Resort zu einem urbanen Zentrum entwickelt und Planer nehmen an, dass es in den nächsten Jahrzehnten um weitere zwei Millionen Zuzügler wachsen wird. Ein solch phänomenales Wachstum eröffnet einer großen Anzahl von Zuwanderern und Heerscharen von „Boosters", den rückhaltlosen Befürwortern der Entwicklung, neue Möglichkeiten. In vielfacher Hinsicht bietet Las Vegas ein hoch entwickeltes städtisches Umfeld: hier finden sich Unterhaltung und Erholung für höchste Ansprüche und ein breites Spektrum an Lifestyle-orientierten Restaurants und Geschäften. Somit ist es eine komplexe Stadt des 21. Jahrhunderts. Doch zugleich ist Las Vegas eine simple Boomtown und dadurch in der Tradition vieler anderer Städte der westlichen Vereinigten Staaten verankert; Städte, deren rasches Wachstum auf dem Abbau von Bodenschätzen beruhte und die viele anzogen, die auf schnellen Reichtum hofften, ohne sich um die sozialen und umweltbezogenen Folgekosten zu bekümmern. Die expansionistische Ideologie des „Manifest Destiny", des Glaubens des 19. Jahrhunderts, dass Amerika dazu bestimmt sei, westwärts zum Pazifik hin zu wachsen, scheint durch den Glauben des 21. Jahrhunderts an das unendliche Wachstum von Touristen-zielen ersetzt worden zu sein. Doch, so erinnert uns die Historikerin Patricia Limerick, wir sollten nicht nur von den Erfolgen der Urbanisierung lernen, sondern auch von den „Landschaften des Scheiterns".[1] Ihre Mahnung wirft die Frage nach den zugrundeliegenden Kriterien auf: Was macht Stadtentwicklung erfolgreich oder lässt sie scheitern und wie sieht dieses Scheitern aus? Zahlreich sind die von der Populärkultur vermittelten Bilder eines strahlenden Las Vegas. Weitgehend unbekannt dagegen sind diejenigen der alltäglichen Welt dieses Wüstentales: die Brüche, Ränder und Infrastrukturen, die nicht leicht mit dieser leuchtenden Stadt vereinbar sind.

Las Vegas birgt eine Vielzahl solcher Landschaften des Scheiterns: die räumlichen und physischen Manifestationen sozialer, kultureller und ökonomischer Praktiken, die ohne Rücksicht auf den Verlust kultureller Erinnerung und Identität oder die Zerrüttung und Zerstörung lebensfähiger sozialer und kultureller Netzwerke von neuen Praktiken kurzerhand beiseite geschoben wurden. Heute kann das Las Vegas, das von Robert Venturi und Denise Scott Brown gefeiert wurde, die Stadt, deren Mythos untrennbar mit dem Rat Pack, mit Howard Hughes und Elvis Presley verbunden ist, nur noch im Rückblick gepriesen werden. Berühmte Kasinos der Vergangenheit wurden abgerissen und die mit ihnen verbundenen Erinnerungen mit der gleichen Leichtigkeit zur Seite gefegt, mit der die Trailer-Parks ausgelöscht

Sites of Transition:
Urbanizing the Mojave Desert

This book documents processes of urbanization in the Las Vegas Valley and the Mojave Desert beyond the well-known spectacles of the Las Vegas Strip. With a greater metropolitan area encompassing more than two million residents, Las Vegas has transformed from a desert resort to an urban center and planners expect it to grow by yet another two million newcomers in the coming decades. Such phenomenal expansion has provided opportunity for great numbers of newcomers and the city's boosters are legion. It is a profoundly sophisticated urban environment, combining high-end entertainment and recreation with the dining and shopping opportunities associated with "lifestyle" economies. As such it is a complex twenty-first century city. However, Las Vegas is also a simple boomtown and, in this manner, it is anchored in the tradition of many other cities in the western United States; cities that have grown quickly on the basis of extractive industries with multitudes coming to strike it rich without attending to the final social or environmental costs. The expansionist ideology of Manifest Destiny, the nineteenth-century belief that America was destined to grow westwards towards the Pacific, may truly be superseded by a twenty-first century belief in the endless growth of tourist destinations. However, as the western historian Patricia Limerick reminds us, we need to learn not only from the successes of urbanization, but also from the "Landscape of Failure."[1] Her reminder raises the question about underlying criteria: what makes urban development succeed or fail, and what might this look like? Images of a radiantly successful Las Vegas are abundantly evident in many forms of popular culture. Largely unknown are those of the everyday world of this desert valley: the breaks, edges, and infrastructures not so easily reconciled with images of the luminous city.

Las Vegas contains numerous landscapes of apparent failure: the spatial and physical manifestations of social, cultural, and economic practices quickly swept aside by new practices without regard to loss of cultural memory and identity, or to the disruption and destruction of viable social and cultural networks. Thus the Las Vegas celebrated by Robert Venturi and Denise Scott Brown, or mythologized by the Rat Pack, Howard Hughes and Elvis Presley, can now only be eulogized. Famed casinos of the past have been imploded and their memories swept aside with the same ease as the trailer parks that are erased for access to land of skyrocketing value. At Chicago's Columbia World Exposition of 1893, the historian Frederick Jackson Turner established the "Significance of the American Frontier," defined it as the "meeting point between savagery and civilization," and declared its closure.[2] In today's Las Vegas, the "New Frontier," one of the few survivors of the original Strip casinos, was demolished to make way for a multi-billion dollar

werden, um Bauland mit rasant steigendem Wert zu erschließen. Auf der Chicagoer Weltausstellung von 1893 konstatierte der Historiker Frederick Jackson Turner die „Bedeutung der Amerikanischen Grenze", an der „Barbarei und Zivilisation" aufeinanderträfen, und erklärte ihre Schließung.[2] Im heutigen Las Vegas wurde das „New Frontier", eines der letzten übrig gebliebenen originalen Kasinos am Strip, abgerissen, um Platz für das mehrere Milliarden schwere „French Renaissance" Resort zu schaffen, für das das New York City Plaza Hotel als Vorbild diente.[3] Dieses ironische Echo auf die Beaux-Arts-Kreationen der Weltausstellung unterstreicht die Schließung der Stadt, die Venturi und Scott Brown so faszinierte. Auf gleiche Weise löscht der derzeit im Bau befindliche extravagante CityCenter-Complex am Strip, der als Neun-Milliarden-Dollar-Projekt mit dem Etikett „Into the New" vermarktet wird, das frühere Las Vegas aus. In einer Umgebung, in der viele um die Zukunft wetten, um sich für die Verluste der Vergangenheit zu entschädigen, sind die Einsätze überaus hoch. Patricia Limerick hat bemerkt, dass der amerikanische Westen „lange Zeit Heimat für einen Kult der Ruinen war", doch dies gilt nicht für Las Vegas. Bei einem solchen Verlust an kollektivem Gedächtnis ist es nur passend, dass das erste Gebäude, das ein Stararchitekt für Las Vegas entworfen hat, das Lou-Ruvo-Institut von Frank Gehry, der Erforschung der Alzheimer-Krankheit gewidmet ist.

Somit kann von drei Dichotomien gesprochen werden, die Las Vegas prägen: der des Strip und der ihn umgebenden Stadt, derjenigen von Landschaften des Erfolgs und des Scheiterns, und derjenigen der Auslöschung der Vergangenheit auf der Suche nach einer immer neuen Zukunft. Eine vierte Dichotomie ist ebenfalls wesentlich, um unsere Fotodokumentation zu verstehen: die grundlegende Spannung zwischen den Prozessen der Urbanisierung in einer extremen und extrem fragilen Umgebung und der Landschaft, in der sich diese Prozesse entfaltet haben. Die Neuauflage der Mojave-Wüste als spektakuläre Wohnenklave eines „Roma Hills" oder „Lake Las Vegas" spiegelt die Entwicklungen des Strip, während das „Crystal Ridge"-Projekt die massiven Eingriffe nachahmt, die mit dem Bergbau verbunden werden. Zusammen mit der Tendenz endlosen Sprawls bewirken sie eine Auslöschung, die auch die Identität der Mojave-Wüste selbst betrifft.

Wir erinnern uns, dass Venturi und Scott Brown ihre einflussreiche Untersuchung des Strip als einer neuen Form der Urbanisierung 1968 begannen.[4] Im selben Jahr startete der britische Architekturhistoriker und Kritiker Reyner Banham (1922–1988) von seiner zeitweiligen Wahlheimat Los Angeles aus seine Streifzüge in die Mojave-Wüste, die er in seinen *Scenes in America Deserta* (1982) beschrieb. Während Venturi

"French Renaissance" resort modeled on New York City's Plaza Hotel.[3] This ironic echo of the beaux-arts creations of the World Exposition underscores the closure of the city that had so fascinated Venturi and Scott Brown. Similarly erasing the former Las Vegas, the Strip's extravagant "CityCenter" complex now under construction is a seven billion dollar project marketed with the tagline "Into the New." In an environment in which many gamble on the future in order to recoup the loss of the past, the stakes are exceedingly high. Limerick has noted that the American West "has long been home to a cult of ruins," but this has no place in the Las Vegas Valley. With such a loss of urban collective memory, it is fitting that Las Vegas's first building by a signature architect is the Lou Ruvo Institute, designed by Frank Gehry and dedicated to the study of Alzheimer's disease.

Thus one can speak of three dichotomies: the Strip and the surrounding city, the landscapes of success and failure, and the erasure of the past in search of an ever-new future. A fourth dichotomy is also essential to understanding our photo-documentation: the profound tension between the processes of urbanization in an extreme and extremely fragile environment and the landscape in which these processes have unfolded. Remaking the Mojave Desert into spectacular residential enclaves such as "Roma Hills" and "Lake Las Vegas" mirrors Strip developments while the Crystal Ridge project most closely mimics the massive interventions associated with mining. Coupled with the tendency towards endless sprawl, these too invoke erasure, erasing the identity of the Mojave Desert itself.

We are reminded that Venturi and Scott Brown began their seminal examination of the Strip as a new form of urbanization in 1968.[4] That same year Reyner Banham (1922–1988), the British architectural historian and critic, began making forays into the Mojave Desert from his temporary home in Los Angeles, forays he described in his *Scenes in America Deserta* (1982). Whereas Venturi and Scott Brown relied heavily on semiotics in their urban analysis, helping to usher in architectural postmodernism, Banham engaged the desert as a highly abstract, modernist environment. For him, this environment wasn't understood in terms of signs and symbols, but in terms of light, shadow, form and space.

Although the desert is surprisingly present in many of Venturi and Scott Brown's photographs of the early Strip, they kept their frame of reference closely cropped. Their focus was on the Strip and its architecture, avoiding the desert. Banham focused on the desert, avoiding the city. In their respective works a dualism is implied: the city as presence, the desert as absence. Banham even quotes Frank Lloyd Wright, who had constructed his own winter camp in the desert a few hundred miles to the east: "The

Las Vegas "Strip" 1963

und Scott Brown sich in ihrer Stadtanalyse an der Semiotik orientierten und damit dazu beitrugen, die architektonische Postmoderne einzuleiten, sah Banham die Wüste als hochgradig abstrakte, modernistische Umgebung. Für ihn war diese Umgebung nicht im Sinn von Zeichen und Symbolen zu verstehen, sondern in dem von Licht, Schatten, Form und Raum.

Obwohl die Wüste in vielen von Venturis und Scott Browns Fotografien überraschend präsent ist, fassten sie doch ihren Bezugsrahmen eng. Ihr Fokus war, die Wüste meidend, auf den Strip und seine Architektur gerichtet. Banham fokussierte die Wüste und vermied die Stadt. In ihren jeweiligen Arbeiten ist ein Dualismus angelegt: gilt die Stadt als das Anwesende, so gilt die Wüste als das Abwesende, und Banham zitiert sogar Frank Lloyd Wright, der sein eigenes Winterlager einige hundert Meilen weiter östlich in der Wüste aufgeschlagen hatte: „Die Wüste ist, wo Gott ist und der Mensch nicht ist."[5] Banham verschiebt seinen Fokus jedoch schnell zur Wüste als Quelle ästhetischen, besonders „visuellen Genusses".[6] Er war zutiefst davon beeindruckt, wie das Licht „geradewegs durch das Auge" hindurchgeht und suchte die rauschhafte Erfahrung „unvermittelter ästhetischer Resonanz".[7] Wie John Beck bemerkte, artikuliert Banham eine „nicht-instrumentalisierende Sicht auf die Wüste als den großen Verweigerer: ihre Pracht beruht auf der Unmöglichkeit, sie zu fassen. Die Wüste ist jenseits ... der Vernunft und deshalb nicht innerhalb der Begriffe eines restriktiven rationalen Denkens fassbar."[8] Den Blick ausschließlich auf die ästhetischen Qualitäten der Wüste gerichtet, umging Banham das „verrückte Stadtbild von Las Vegas."[9]

Zum Verständnis dieser Spannung zwischen den Prozessen explosionsartigen Stadtwachstums und den steigenden Belastungen, die dieses Wachstum für die Mojave-Wüste bedeutet, bedarf es komplexerer Begriffe als jener der Anti-Sprawl-Politik: So kann sie als die Spannung zwischen einer Umwelt der Zeichen und Symbole einerseits und einer Umwelt von Raum und Licht andererseits gesehen werden oder als Spannung zwischen postmodernistischer und modernistischer Landschaft. Dieser Spannung entspricht eine klare Dichotomie repräsentativer Systeme: die von Venturi und Scott Brown produzierten filmischen und fotografischen Abbildungen formulieren Themen, die sich sehr von denen unterscheiden, die normalerweise mit Darstellungen des amerikanischen Westens verbunden werden. Es ist wichtig, das, was auf dem Spiel steht, im Hinblick auf diese verschiedenartigen Repräsentationssysteme zu verstehen.

So ist *Learning from Las Vegas* beispielsweise an den filmischen Wahrnehmungen der modernen (autogerechten) Stadt orientiert, wie sie der Städtebauer Kevin Lynch entwickelte. Lynch glaubte, dass ein filmi-

desert is where God is and man is not."[5] However, Banham quickly shifts focus to the desert as a source of aesthetic pleasure, specifically "visual pleasure."[6] He was struck by the kind of light that goes "straight through the eye" and drawn toward the rapture of "an unmediated aesthetic response."[7] As John Beck has written, Banham articulates a "noninstrumental view of the desert as the great refuser: its physical splendor lies in the impossibility of grasping it. The desert is ... beyond reason and therefore not recuperable within the terms of restrictive rational thought."[8] With his focus on the aesthetic qualities of the desert, Banham bypassed the "mad townscape of Las Vegas."[9]

The tension between the processes of explosive urban growth and the increasing strain this growth places on the Mojave Desert can be understood in terms more complex than those simply arising from the politics of anti-sprawl: it can be understood as an environment of signs and symbols versus one of space and light, and as a postmodernist versus a modernist landscape. This tension is paralleled by a clear dichotomy in representational systems: the filmic and photographic imagery produced by Venturi and Scott Brown frame issues very different than those generally associated with representations of the American west. It is important to understand what is at stake with regard to these diverse representational systems.

For example, *Learning from Las Vegas*, draws from the "filmic" perceptions of the modern (vehicular) city addressed by the urbanist Kevin Lynch. Lynch felt that a filmic approach was key to comprehending the scale and order of uncontrolled, sprawling cities and, in 1953, he argued for analyzing the perceptual form of the city by documenting freeway drives through photography, motion pictures, and written descriptions. Together with Donald Appleyard and John Meyer, Lynch published *The View from the Road* (1964), insisting that the road was the "best means of re-establishing coherence and order on a new metropolitan scale."[10] Agitating less against the physical disorder of decentralization and sprawl than against the visual disorder engendered by proliferating signage, they hoped to develop a new visual "order" based on the "moving view" experienced by car.[11] Considering the "sense of driving a car" as akin to the cinema, the use of film was recommended for documentary and design purposes.[12] One suggested approach was their "Space-Motion and View Diagram," a map representing the ways in which the "space-motion combination" was to "direct the eye."[13] Based on this study, Venturi and Scott Brown conducted the analyses of what Fred Koetter called the Strip's "electrographic 'view from the road'."[14] In addition to such filmic analyses, *Learning from Las Vegas* draws heavily from the photography of late-1950s British pop culture and its migration

scher Ansatz grundlegend war, um den Maßstab und die Ordnung unkontrolliert sich ausbreitender Städte zu begreifen, und argumentierte 1953 dafür, diese Wahrnehmungsform der Stadt zu analysieren, indem man Autobahnfahrten anhand einer Kombination von Fotografien, Filmen und schriftlichen Beschreibungen dokumentierte. Zusammen mit Donald Appleyard und John Meyer publizierte Lynch später die Studie *The View from the Road* (1964), in der er betonte, dass die Straße das „beste Mittel [sei], um Zusammenhang und Ordnung in einem neuen metropolitanen Maßstab herzustellen."[10] Hier ereiferten sie sich weniger über die physische Unordnung von Dezentralisierung und Sprawl, sondern über die visuelle Unordnung sich wildwuchsartig ausbreitender Schilder und hofften, eine neue visuelle Ordnung zu entwickeln, die auf dem „bewegten Blick" des Autofahrers basieren sollte.[11] Da sie die „Empfindung des Fahrens" als der des Kinos gleichartig ansahen, rieten sie dazu, Film zu Dokumentations- und Entwurfszwecken einzusetzen.[12] Einer dieser kinematografischen Ansätze war ihr „Space-Motion and View Diagram", eine Karte, die darstellte, wie die „Kombination von Raum und Bewegung" das Auge „leiten" sollte.[13] Auf der Grundlage dieser Studie führten Venturi und Scott Brown ihre Analyse des Strip durch, die Fred Koetter als „elektrografischen Blick von der Straße" bezeichnete.[14]

Neben solch filmischen Analysen orientierte sich *Learning from Las Vegas* stark an der Fotografie der britischen Popkultur der späten 1950er Jahre und ihres Transfers in die Staaten sowie an den Fotografen Ed Ruscha und später Stephen Shore, dessen *Uncommon Places* von Venturi hohes Lob empfing. Das gesteigerte Interesse an der Popkultur verdankt sich auch Scott Brown, die als Architekturstudentin im London der 50er Jahre mit der *Independent Group* in Berührung kam. Diese Gruppe von Architekten und Designern glaubte, dass der Wert der Kunst nicht in dem lag, *was* sie bedeutete, sondern in ihrer *Fähigkeit zu bedeuten* und an einem System von Bedeutungszuweisungen teilzunehmen. Dieser Glaube wurde auf alle Formen kultureller Produktion übertragen, um die Trennungen zwischen hoher und niederer Kunst zu überwinden. Die Tilgung dieser Trennung erlaubte es der *Independent Group,* aus eklektischen Quellen wie Werbung, Beschilderung, Kino und kinematografischen Praktiken zu schöpfen.

Banhams Verbindung mit der *Independent Group* wird in seinem einflussreichen Buch *Los Angeles: The Architecture of Four Ecologies* (1971) spürbar. Ein Jahr vor der Veröffentlichung von *Learning from Las Vegas* betonte Banham hier, dass „in Los Angeles die Sprache von Design, Architektur und Städtebau die Sprache der Bewegung ist" und fügte hinzu,

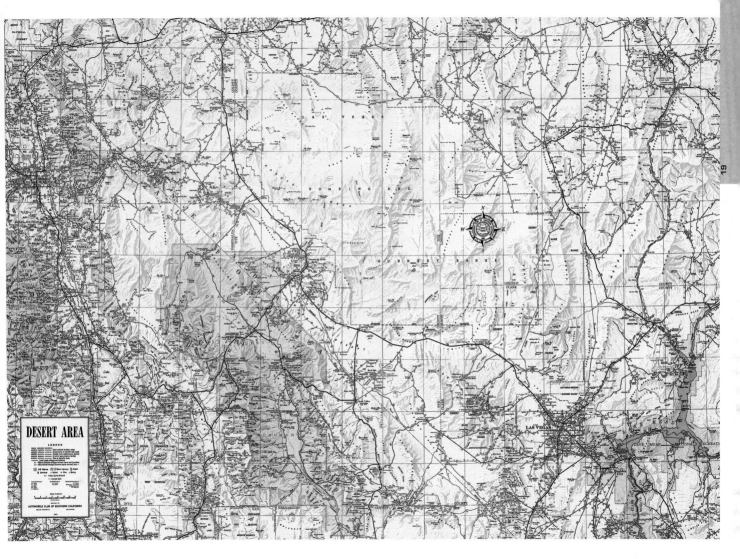

dass er „fahren lerne, um Los Angeles im Original zu lesen".[15] Diese Argumentation deckt sich mit der Lynchs und seiner Nachfolger, und sicherlich folgten ihm sein Interesse an Autobahnen und Bewegung sowie seine Erfahrungen als „Voyeur auf Rädern" in die Wüste.[16] Im Gegensatz zu den Quellen der Film- und Popkultur ist jedoch Banhams Faszination für Raum und Licht der Wüste mit einem anderen Set von Kriterien verbunden, die mit dem Erhabenen assoziiert werden. Als ästhetische Kategorie in einem vom überwältigenden Maßstab und der Kraft ungezähmter Natur faszinierten Europa des 18. Jahrhunderts entstanden, prägte das Erhabene viele der Darstellungen des amerikanischen Westens im 19. und 20. Jahrhundert, etwa die Gemälde von Frederic Church (1826–1900), Albert Bierstadt (1830–1902) und Thomas Moran (1837–1926); Fotografien von Carleton Watkins (1829–1916), Timothy O'Sullivan (1840–1882) und Anselm Adams (1902–1984); oder die Kinematografie des Westerns von John Ford (1894–1973), William Wellman (1896–1975) und Anthony Mann (b. Emil Bundesmann, 1906–1967). Indem sie Orte vom Death Valley bis zum Monument Valley, von den Grand Tetons bis zum Grand Canyon abbildeten, trugen diese Darstellungen unermesslich zur Erfindung und Konstruktion des amerikanischen Westens bei und konstituierten einen wesentlichen Teil des amerikanischen kulturellen Gedächtnisses.

Banham war außerdem ein Bewunderer von John C. Van Dyke, eines Kunsthistorikers, der als Asthmaopfer des 19. Jahrhunderts in der Wüste Linderung suchte.[17] 1901 publizierte dieser einen Bericht über seine Erfahrungen mit dem Titel *The Desert: Further Studies in Natural Appearances*, in dem die Wüste erhabene Gestalt erlangt: „Sie hat nichts, das ‚schön' wäre und nicht einen Fleck, der ‚malerisch' ist … Sie ist hart, harsch und auf den ersten Blick abstoßend. Aber welche Sprache soll von ihrer Majestät berichten, von ihrer ewigen Kraft, der Poesie ihres ausgedehnten Chaos, der Erhabenheit ihrer einsamen Ödnis!"[18] Diese Empfindung hallt in Banhams Worten wider, wenn er betont, dass die „Wüste messbar unmessbaren Raum darbietet" und hinzufügt, dass sie deshalb eine Umgebung ist, „in der sich der ‚moderne Mensch' zuhause fühlen sollte – seine moderne Malerei, wie in den Werken Mondrians, impliziert einen Raum, der sich über die Grenzen der Leinwand ausdehnt; seine moderne Architektur, wie in den Werken Mies van der Rohes, ist eine rechtwinklige Wiederholung eines regelmäßigen, jedoch unendlichen Raumes; seine idealen Bewohner pirschen metaphysisch durch den sich endlos erstreckenden Raum."[19] Hier, in dieser „großen Stille" des unendlichen Raumes der Wüste ist wenig Platz für das raue semiotische Tingeltangel und die Architektur des Straßenrandes, die Venturi und Scott Brown so faszinierte.

to America, as well as from the photographic work of Ed Ruscha and, later, Stephen Shore, whose *Uncommon Places* received high praise from Venturi. The interest in Pop owes much to Scott Brown who, as an architectural student in 1950s London, was exposed to the *Independent Group,* a group of architects and designers that believed the value in art lay not in *what* it signified, but in its *ability to* signify and participate in a system of signification. This belief was extended to all forms of cultural production, with the aim of overcoming divisions between high and low art. Erasing these divisions allowed the *Independent Group* to appropriate from eclectic sources, including advertising, signage, cinema, and cinematic practices.

Banham, too, was associated with the *Independent Group* and its influence is felt in his seminal *Los Angeles: The Architecture of Four Ecologies* (1971), published the year before *Learning from Las Vegas.* In this book Banham insisted that the "language of design, architecture, and urbanism in Los Angeles is the language of movement," adding that he "learned to drive in order to read Los Angeles in the original."[15] This argumentation aligns him with Lynch, his interest in freeways and movement following him into his desert experiences as a "wheeled *voyeur.*"[16] However, in contrast to filmic and pop sources, Banham's fascination with desert space and light are linked to another set of criteria, those associated with the sublime. Arising as an aesthetic category in an eighteenth-century Europe fascinated with the overwhelming scale and power of untamed nature, the natural sublime framed many nineteenth- and twentieth-century representations of the American west. Such representations include paintings by Frederic Church (1826–1900), Albert Bierstadt (1830–1902), and Thomas Moran (1837–1926); photography by Carleton Watkins (1829–1916), Timothy O'Sullivan (1840–1882), and Ansel Adams (1902–1984); or the cinematography in westerns by John Ford (1894–1973), William Wellman (1896–1975), and Anthony Mann (b. Emil Bundesmann, 1906–1967). Imaging sites from Death Valley to Monument Valley, the Grand Tetons to the Grand Canyon, these representations have contributed immeasurably to the invention and construction of the American west and constitute a fundamental part of American cultural memory.

Banham was also an *aficionado* of John C. Van Dyke, a professor of art history who, as a nineteenth-century victim of asthma, sought relief in the desert.[17] In 1901 Van Dyke published an account of his experiences, entitled *The Desert: Further Studies in Natural Appearances* and here the desert is redolent of the sublime: "There is not a thing about it that is 'pretty,' and not a spot upon it that is 'picturesque' ... It is stern, harsh, and at first repellent. But what tongue shall tell the majesty of it, the eternal strength

Aus diesem Grund bewegten wir uns für *Die Urbanisierung der Mojave-Wüste: Las Vegas* bildlich zwischen Pop und Kino, Semiotik und dem Erhabenen, während wir das Las Vegas Valley durchquerten. So glitten wir die Hauptverkehrsadern der Stadt entlang, von Norden nach Süden und Osten nach Westen, vorbei an den endlosen Betonstein-Wänden der „Big-Box-Gebäude" und der *gated communities*, die an ihren Rändern Wache stehen, und immer wieder überrascht von den schnellen Übergängen zwischen solch eng begrenzten Räumen und der Weite noch immer größtenteils unberührter Landstriche in Bundesbesitz, Naturschutzgebiete und Nationalparks, die die Stadt umgeben. Allmähliche Übergänge sind selten, und die raschen Wechsel von Wahrnehmungsweisen und Möglichkeiten der Darstellung beeindruckten uns tief. Die oft krassen Gegensätze waren schwierig zu vermitteln und riefen mehr Fragen als Antworten hervor: es fiel uns schwer, das grelle, pulsierende Neon mit der Wärme des Wüstenlichts zu versöhnen, das über Red Rock Canyon und den Spring Mountains im Westen auf- oder über Frenchman Mountain und den Rainbow Gardens im Osten unterging. (S. 107, 112, 145) In Anbetracht einer solch spektakulären natürlichen Umgebung war es gleichermaßen schwierig, den Anblick neu erschlossener Gebiete mit ihren neuen Namen – viele von ihnen italienischer Herkunft – in Einklang zu bringen; die Verlagerung der Toskana, des Veneto oder der römischen Campagna auf den gebüschbedeckten Boden des Las Vegas Valley oder das Umtaufen jener Yucca-bedeckten Hügel auf den Namen italienischer Inseln oder französischer Gärten. (S. 171, 173) Hier wird der erhabene Westen von Frederic Church, Timothy O'Sullivan und Henry Ford in eine Grand Tour von Bädern und Golfplätzen verwandelt, die dem Geiste Fellinis entsprungen zu sein scheint.

In der Innenstadt waren diese Orte des Übergangs in den Gebieten am offensichtlichsten, die, einst von marginaler wirtschaftlicher Bedeutung, nun unter enormem Entwicklungsdruck standen. Die Plötzlichkeit, mit der infolgedessen die Trailer-Parks, die älteren Nachbarschaften mit kleineren Häusern auf größeren Grundstücken oder sogar ältere Kasinos verschwanden, war bemerkenswert. (S. 120, 121) Oftmals wurden im Zeitraum weniger Wochen eine große Anzahl der von uns dokumentierten Bauten der gigantischen Mülldeponie übergeben, die an den nördlichen Randgebieten der Stadt liegt. Als gleichermaßen vergänglich und kurzlebig erwies sich die Beschilderung, besonders die Schilder, die mit Bauprojekten verbunden waren, erschienen und verschwanden in rascher Folge. (S. 86) Dies traf für die innerstädtische und die periphere Entwicklung gleichermaßen zu. Am beeindruckendsten von allem war jedoch die plötzliche Überlagerung unberührter Umgebungen mit massiv in die Landschaft eingreifenden Entwicklungspro-

of it, the poetry of its wide-spread chaos, the sublimity of its lonely desolation!"[18] Banham echoed this sentiment, insisting that the "desert measurably offers immeasurable space," adding that it "is therefore an environment in which 'Modern Man' ought to feel at home – his modern painting, as in the works of Mondrian, implies a space that extends beyond the confines of the canvas; his modern architecture, as in the works of Mies van der Rohe, is a rectangular petition of a regular but infinite space; its ideal inhabitants stalking metaphysically through that space as far as it infinitely extends."[19] Here, in the "great silence" of the desert's infinite space, there is little place for the raucous semiotic honky-tonk and roadside architecture that so fascinated Venturi and Scott Brown.

Therefore, in undertaking *Urbanizing the Mojave Desert: Las Vegas,* we moved metaphorically between pop and cinema, semiotics and the sublime as we traversed the Las Vegas Valley. Gliding through the city along major arteries from north to south and east to west, their edges tautly guarded by the endless concrete block walls of "big box" buildings and gated communities, the greatest surprises were always associated with the rapid transition from such narrowly bounded spaces to the vastness of the still largely pristine federal lands, conservation areas and National Parks surrounding the city. Gradual transitions are few and we were continually struck by the rapid shifts in modes of perception and the possibilities of representation. Negotiating the often stark differences of this transition was difficult and always raised more questions than answers: we could not reconcile the pulse of bright neon with the warmth of desert light rising on Red Rock Canyon and the Spring Mountains to the west or setting on Frenchman Mountain and the Rainbow Gardens to the east. (pp. 107, 112, 145) Given such a spectacular physical environment, it was equally difficult to reconcile the sight of new place names, a great many of Italian origin, with the sites of new developments; the displacing of the Toscana, Veneto or Roman Campagna to the greasewood floor of the Las Vegas Valley, or the rechristening of yucca-covered hillsides as Italian islands or French gardens. (pp. 171, 173) Here the sublime west of Church, O'Sullivan and Ford is transformed into a Felliniesque Grand Tour of golf courses and spas.

In the inner city, signs of sites in transition were most in evidence in areas of marginal economic importance now under great development pressures. The resulting and very sudden disappearance of trailer parks, older communities of smaller homes on larger properties, or even older casinos, was striking, often occurring within a few weeks. (pp. 120, 121) A great number of the structures we have documented have since been consigned to the gigantic landfill located on the northern outskirts of the

jekten. (S. 177–79) Der Einsatz schweren Geräts, wie es im Bergbau verwendet wird, rief mit großmaßstäblichen und abstrakten Geometrien eine vorübergehende Schönheit hervor und erfüllte damit vielleicht das Versprechen modernistischer Empfindsamkeiten an Raum und Form. (S. 150, 154, 156–61) Was jedoch folgte, war jeweils ein Feld repetitiver Bauten, die viele der Fehler wiederholen, die dem industrialisierten Bauen der Nachkriegszeit zugeschrieben werden. (S. 166, 167, 180, 181)

Den verstörendsten Anblick boten aber jene Orte jenseits der Peripherie des Valley, die die Vorstöße der Projektentwickler in immer entferntere Abschnitte der Mojave-Wüste bezeugen. Wir fühlten uns an William Fox's einfühlsame Beobachtung erinnert, dass „wir als Spezies nicht dazu ausgerüstet sind, in der Wüste zu funktionieren. In solchen Landschaften verlieren wir unseren Sinn für den physischen Maßstab und die Perspektive, was eine Kluft zwischen dem, was wir zu sehen glauben und der Realität eröffnet [...] der Strip nutzt diese Kluft so weit aus, wie es die Imagination erlaubt."[20] Diese Beobachtung trifft genauso für die Entwicklung jenseits des Strip zu. Heute findet sich kaum noch etwas von der alltäglichen „Budenarchitektur" an den Straßenrändern; stattdessen werden wir Zeugen großmaßstäblicher Interventionen, die nicht mehr von der Erhabenheit des Lichtes und Raumes der Wüste, der großen Stille sprechen, sondern – wenn überhaupt von

irgendetwas – von der scheinbar unendlichen Reichweite und dem Spektakel des globalen Kapitals. Und es stellt sich die dringende Frage, ob diese Interventionen, die gewaltige Mengen an Fläche und Material verschlingen, das kulturelle Versprechen einlösen, das mit der Urbanisierung verbunden wird, oder ob sie lediglich eine neue, gigantische Variation eines alten Themas bilden: der Landschaften des Scheiterns.

city. Signage proved to be equally transitory and ephemeral: signs announcing the development of single buildings or even entire developments appeared and disappeared with great speed, a characteristic of both inner-city and peripheral development. (p. 86) Most striking of all, however, was the sudden overlay of massive, heavily interventionist developments onto pristine environments. (pp. 177–79) Employing the same massive equipment used by the extractive industries, these evoked a passing beauty in their scale and abstract geometries, and perhaps in this manner fulfilled the promise of modernist sensibilities in space and form. (pp. 150, 154, 156–61) What followed, however, was invariably a field of repetitive structures, replicating many of the failures identified with industrialized building in the postwar years. (pp. 166, 167, 180, 181)

Finally, moving beyond the valley's periphery, the most disturbing sites were those of the many incursions by developers ever deeper into the Mojave. We were reminded of William Fox's perceptive observation that "as a species we're not well equipped to function in the desert. We lose our sense of physical scale and perspective in such landscapes, which opens a gap between what we think we are seeing and the reality ... the Strip exploits that gap as far as our imagination will allow."[20] This observation is just as valid for much of the development beyond the Strip. Today one encounters little of the honky-tonk of a roadside vernacular, but is witness to large-scale interventions that, if anything, speak not of the sublimity of desert light and space, of the great silence, but of the seemingly infinite reach and spectacle of global capital. Perhaps most pressing is the question as to whether such massive interventions, both in terms of acreage subsumed and materials consumed, fulfills the cultural promise associated with urbanization or simply constitutes a new and alarming variation on the older themes of a landscape of failure.

Landschaften des Erfolgs, Landschaften des Scheiterns: Die Orte der Ausbeutung, Militarisierung und Erholung

Wie wir gesehen haben, erscheinen die Wüsten des amerikanischen Westens als Landschaften von Dichotomien, die oft so extrem sind wie die Landschaft selbst. Die Mojave verkörpert den räumlichen Zwiespalt zwischen „Strip" und Stadt, Stadt und Wüste, Vergangenheit und Zukunft, Moderne und Postmoderne, Erfolg und Scheitern. Historiker des amerikanischen Westens thematisierten die konzeptuellen Dichotomien, die der Konstruktion des „Westens" zugrunde liegen: „alter Westen" gegen „neuer Westen", „Grenze" gegen „Region", Exzeptionalismus gegen Nationalismus, Individualismus und Triumphalismus gegen Kollektivismus. Viele der daraus hervorgegangenen Wellen der Forschung und Diskussion speisten sich aus Jackson Turners einflussreicher These von „Barbarei gegen Zivilisation". David Wrobel wendet jedoch ein, dass diese Beiträge „ein Jahrhundert der Forschung über den Westen nicht besser repräsentieren als die ‚Cowboys und Indianer'-Dichotomie die Realität des Westens vor einem Jahrhundert".[21]

Wir sind zwar keine Historiker des amerikanischen Westens, doch aufmerksam gegenüber den Fallen unnötiger Einteilungen. Mit *Die Urbanisierung der Mojave-Wüste: Las Vegas* wollen wir Dichotomien wie die von Industrialismus bzw. industriellem Tourismus und Umweltschutz nicht wiederholen. In der Tat untergräbt die Reihe der oben genannten Gegensatzpaare, die sich beständig überlappen und überschneiden, jede Reduktion auf

ein einfaches „dieses oder jenes". Die in diesem Buch gezeigten Bilder verweisen auf die komplexen Prozesse des Übergangs und werfen damit eher Fragen nach den diese Prozesse antreibenden Mechanismen und Kräften auf, als spezifische Antworten zu geben. Wenn der Diskussion, zu der die Abbildungen beitragen, mehr Tiefe verliehen werden soll, ist es wichtig, ein Spektrum von „Orten" zu skizzieren, die mit den Übergängen im zunehmend verstädternden Westen assoziiert werden: Orte der Ausbeutung, Militarisierung und Erholung. Dieses Terrain wird Historikern des Westens sehr vertraut sein; für andere mag es Zugang zu einem Land bieten, in dem pure visuelle Kraft oftmals komplexe Beziehungen verbirgt.

John Beck erinnert daran, dass die Wüste in christlichen und hebräischen Traditionen als Ort der „Jenseitigkeit" gezeichnet wird, als ein Raum der „Leere", der dergestalt einen erstklassigen „Ort ungehinderten Experimentierens, ein zugleich physisches und spirituelles Versuchsfeld" darstellt.[22] Als solches wird die Wüste entweder ein Ort der „Flucht vor der Moderne, eine elementare Alternative zu der rationalen Ordnung ‚zivilisierten' Lebens" oder, so Beck, „repräsentativ für das Chaos einer ungeordneten primitiven ‚Natur', der widerstanden und die gereinigt werden muss [...] Da die amerikanische Wüste in dem ökonomisch aufstrebenden ‚Neuen Westen' der Nachkriegszeit liegt, kann sie zunehmend als repräsentativ für

Landscapes of Success, Landscapes of Failure:
The Sites of Extraction, Militarization, and Recreation

The deserts of the American west appear to be lands of dichotomies, often as stark as the landscape itself. The physical disunion of Strip and city, city and desert, past and future, modern and postmodern, success and failure is to be found in the Mojave. Historians of America's west have addressed the conceptual dichotomies underlying the construction of the "west" itself: "old west" versus "new west," "frontier" versus "region," exceptionalism versus nationalism, individualism and triumphalism versus collectivism. These have generated successive waves of scholarship and argument, much of which has been placed in relation to Frederick Jackson Turner's seminal frontier thesis of "savagery versus civilization." David Wrobel, however, argues that they are "no more representative of a century of scholarship on the West than the 'cowboys and Indians' dichotomy of western reality a century ago."[21]

It is not our intention that *Urbanizing the Mojave Desert: Las Vegas* reiterate dichotomies such as industrialism or industrialized tourism versus environmentalism. Indeed, the series of dichotomies above, which invariably overlap and intersect, undermines the imposition of a simple "this or that." The images in this documentation point to complex processes of transition and raise questions about the mechanisms and forces driving those processes, rather than providing specific answers. It is important to sketch a range of "sites" associated with transitions in the increasingly urban west if greater depth is to be given to the discussion the images are part of: sites of extraction, militarization, and recreation. This terrain will be very familiar to historians of the west; to others it may provide the threshold to a land in which simple visual power often conceals complex interrelationships.

John Beck reminds us that Christian and Hebrew traditions depict the desert as a place of "otherworldliness," as space characterized by "emptiness" and, therefore, a prime "venue for unhindered experimentation, a testing ground both physical and spiritual."[22] As such the desert becomes either a place of "escape from modernity, an elemental alternative to the rational order of 'civilized' life" or, according to Beck, "representative of the chaos of an unordered primal 'nature' that must be resisted and expunged ... as the American desert lies within the economically emergent post–World War II 'New West,' the desert can increasingly be seen as representative of aspects of contemporary capitalism: a space without boundaries, unhindered and unregulated by old practices and habits."[23]

A great deal has been projected into this space "without boundaries, unhindered and unregulated." Sites of transition include places of extraction, militarization and recreation. As mentioned above, sites of extraction stem from both historical and modern eras and their search for mineral wealth,

gewisse Aspekte des zeitgenössischen Kapitalismus gesehen werden: als Raum ohne Grenzen, frei von den Hindernissen oder Regulierungen durch alte Praktiken und Gewohnheiten." [23]

Dieser freie, grenzenlose Raum diente in mannigfacher Weise als Projektionsfläche. Wenn wir von Orten des Übergangs sprechen, bezieht das die Orte der Ausbeutung, Militarisierung und Erholung mit ein. Wie bereits erwähnt, entstammen die Orte der Ausbeutung historischen und modernen Zeiten; der Suche nach Bodenschätzen und den Landschaften des Scheiterns. In Nord-Nevada befanden sich die großen Silbergruben der Comstock Lode, und viele der in Nevada ankommenden Bergarbeiter waren Auswanderer aus Kalifornien; sie siedelten in die Wüste um, als die Vorkommen weiter westlich erschöpft waren – ein Phänomen, das dem heutigen Immobilien-Goldrausch durchaus vergleichbar ist. [24] Nevada ist „also das Land für den ehemaligen Kalifornier [...] plus tausend Prozent dazu", posaunte 1863 die *Gold Hill Daily News*. [25] Wie Eugene Moehring berichtet, erforderten die mit der Ausbeutung des mineralischen Reichtums zusammenhängenden komplexen Abläufe einen „mächtigen industriellen Verbund" mit „Städten an strategischen Punkten." [26] Zusammen umfassten diese ein „urbanes Netzwerk", dessen Herzstück Gold Hill, Silver City und Virginia City bildeten. [27] Aufgrund ihrer Größe und städtischen Komplexität war Virginia City besonders wichtig, hier gab es sogar ein Chinatown mit Industrien, die den Rest der Stadt versorgten. [28] Im Zentrum stark verdichtet, wurde dieses urbane Netzwerk „an seiner Peripherie durch die Bildung anderer Typologien städtischer Orte verlängert, die mit dem Kern durch Straßen, Wege und wirtschaftliche Beziehungen verbunden waren". [29] Zeitgenössische Abbildungen zeigen geschäftige, durcheinandergewürfelte Stadtlandschaften, beherrscht von Abraumhalden und den Schornsteinen der Schmelzereien. Timothy O'Sullivan und William Henry Jackson fotografierten den Bergbau Comstocks und machten die Geschichte dieser Orte zugänglich. Dieses komplexe urbane System kann räumlich als Subsystem beschrieben werden, als „periphere Erweiterung" eines Stadtsystems, das sich infolge des Goldrausches in Kalifornien entwickelt hatte. [30]

Weiter südlich erblühten und verfielen Städte wie Eureka, Tonopah, Goldfield, Rhyolite, Beatty und Manhattan. Obwohl es in Süd-Nevada und der Mojave keine Orte wie Comstock gibt, blieb südlich von Las Vegas mit Goodsprings bis in die Nachkriegszeit eine aktive Bergbausiedlung bestehen. Seine Nähe zu dem Areal, auf dem Las Vegas einen neuen Flughafen errichten wird, wird Goodsprings zu neuem Aufschwung verhelfen.

Westlich hiervon lagen die großen Borax-Minen von Death Valley; berühmt wurde der hier betriebene Abbau des „weißen Goldes" durch die

often resulting in landscapes of failure. Northern Nevada was the site of the great Comstock Lode and, as can also be said for today's real estate bonanza, many of the miners arriving in Nevada belonged to an exodus from California that relocated to the desert as the strikes further west were exhausted.[24] Nevada is, "after all, the land for the old Californian ... with a thousand percent added thereto," trumpeted the *Gold Hill Daily News* in 1863.[25] Eugene Moehring reports that the complex processes associated with extracting great mineral wealth required a "massive industrial system" with "towns at strategic points."[26] Together these comprised an "urban network", whose core consisted of Gold Hill, Silver City, and Virginia City.[27] Virginia City was particularly important in its size and urban complexity; it even developed a Chinatown with industries serving the city.[28] With a dense center, the urban network was "elongated at its periphery by the formation of other types of urban places connected to the core by roads, trails, and economics."[29] Contemporary images depict bustling and jumbled townscapes dominated by mine tailings and the smokestacks of smelters. Both Timothy O'Sullivan and William Henry Jackson photographed mining activities at Comstock, providing a rich visual history of these sites. Spatially, this already complex urban system may be described as a subsystem, a "peripheral extension" of the urban system that originated in California following its Gold Rush.[30]

Further south, cities such as Eureka, Tonopah, Goldfield, Rhyolite, Beatty, and Manhattan flourished and faded. Although there are no major sites like Comstock in southern Nevada and the Mojave, Goodsprings, to the south of Las Vegas, remained an active mining community until the postwar era. Its location, adjacent to the area in which Las Vegas will build a new international airport, will allow Goodsprings to flourish again. To the west there were the great borax mines of Death Valley; this "white gold" mining was popularized with the television series *Death Valley Days* and its host Ronald Reagan. Finally, the city of Henderson was founded directly in what would become the greater Las Vegas metropolitan area to house workers of the Basic Magnesium plant. Built in 1941 to supply magnesium for the war effort, Basic Magnesium employed fully ten percent of Nevada's population. Plant buildings still exist and this brownfield site is being converted to commercial use as a typical strip mall. (p. 152 top right)

In addition to the many ghost towns and collections of industrial debris, many of these sites are marked by substantial tailings and related acid mine drainage (AMD), a condition in which the metal sulfides contained in the residual rock dissolve due to exposure to oxygen and water. They then turn into sulfuric acid and contaminate ground water and runoff. The director of the Mining Life-Cycle Center of the Mackay School of Mines (University of

Fernsehserie *Death Valley Days* und ihren Moderator Ronald Reagan. Zuletzt wurde die Stadt Henderson in der späteren Metropolregion Las Vegas gegründet, um Arbeiter einer Basic-Magnesium-Fabrik unterzubringen. Die 1941 zur Produktion des kriegswichtigen Magnesiums erbaute Fabrik beschäftigte zehn Prozent der Bevölkerung Nevadas. Die noch existierenden Fabrikgebäude werden nun kommerziell genutzt und in ein typisches Einkaufszentrum umgebaut. (Abb. S. 152 oben, rechts)

Zusätzlich zu den vielen Geisterstädten und dem Industrieschutt sind viele dieser Orte durch schlammartige Abraumrückstände, das Tailing, und eine Versauerung der Gewässer gezeichnet. Hierbei lösen sich die metallischen Sulfide im Gestein durch den Kontakt mit Sauerstoff und Wasser auf und verwandeln sich in schwefelhaltige Säure, die Grund- und Abwasser kontaminiert. Der Direktor des Mining Life-Cycle Centers der Mackay School of Mines (University of Nevada Reno) schätzt, dass „fünf Prozent der stillgelegten Minen in irgendeiner Weise Umweltschäden auslösen" und die Environmental Protection Agency (EPA) vermutet, dass etwa „40 Prozent der Wassereinzugsgebiete der westlichen Vereinigten Staaten" von Verschmutzung durch den Bergbau betroffen sind.[31]

Wo Immobilien Bodenschätze ersetzen, ist die aktuelle Urbanisierung unverhofften Heimsuchungen ausgesetzt. In Nevada liegen 225.000 bis 310.000 stillgelegte Minen, von denen 50.000 eine direkte Gefährdung für die Öffentlichkeit darstellen. 1996 wurden die Leichen von zwei Männern in verlassenen Minen gefunden, die aufgrund kohlendioxydgefüllter Hohlräume mit dem Schild „Keep Out – Bad Air" gekennzeichnet waren.[32] 1999 fiel ein elfjähriges Kind nördlich von Las Vegas in einen 60 Meter tiefen Schacht. Hieraus folgerte J. Davitt McAteer, dass „Nevadas Vergangenheit und Gegenwart auf eine Kollision zusteuern" und dass suburbaner Sprawl und stillgelegter Bergbau nicht kompatibel seien.[33] Besonders für Mountainbiker und die Fahrer von Geländewagen birgt das Gebiet heimtückische Gefahren, weil sie leicht in tiefe, ungesicherte Löcher fallen können. 2007 stürzten zwei junge Mädchen auf einer Wochenendfahrt in der Wüste östlich von Las Vegas mit ihrem Geländewagen in einen 40 Meter tiefen Schacht.[34]

Innerhalb des Stadtgebietes lauern andere Gefahren. Weite Flächen des braunfarbenen Las Vegas Valley sind durch beunruhigend grell-grünen Rasen geprägt; die Amerikaner schätzen den Anschein vorstädtischer Adrettheit, den er ihren Vorgärten verleiht. Um Wasser zu sparen, wendet man sich bei neuen Baugebieten jedoch immer mehr dem „Xeriscaping" zu, einer Form der Landschaftsgestaltung, die nur Stein, Kies und dürrebeständige Pflanzen verwendet, die in der Region beheimatet sind. Dass dies nicht ohne Risiko ist, zeigten Fälle, in denen

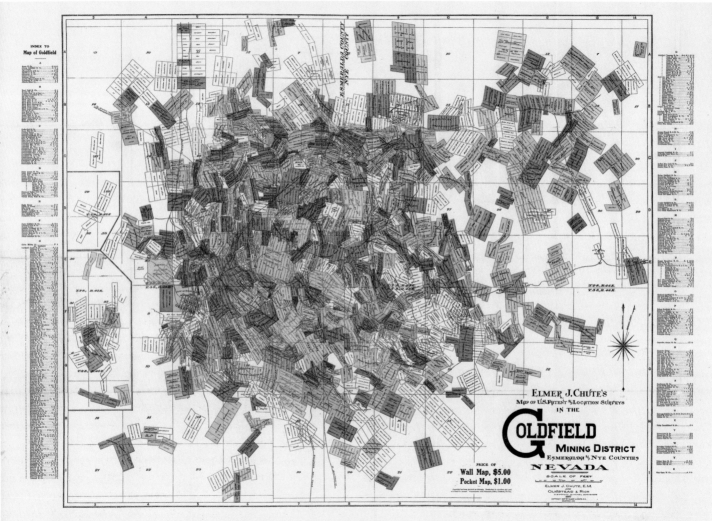

INDEX TO
Map of Goldfield

ELMER J. CHUTE'S
MAP OF U.S. PATENT & LOCATION SURVEYS
IN THE

GOLDFIELD
MINING DISTRICT
ESMERALDA & NYE COUNTIES
NEVADA
SCALE OF FEET

ELMER J. CHUTE, E.M.
AND
OLMSTEAD & RICH

PRICE OF
Wall Map, $5.00
Pocket Map, $1.00

der für Xeriscaping verwendete Stein und Kies von stillgelegten Minen bezogen wurde. Durch die Belastung mit schwefelhaltigen Mineralien birgt diese dekorative Landschaftsgestaltung die Gefahr schwerwiegender Metallvergiftungen, die durch Staubinhalation oder Berührung verursacht werden, sowie weiterer Gesundheitsgefährdungen, wenn die Schadstoffe in die städtische Wasserversorgung gelangen.[35]

Heutzutage wird das Gesicht der Wüste um Las Vegas weniger von der Suche nach wertvollen Chemikalien oder Metallen geprägt als vielmehr von den gewaltigen Kies- und Gipssteinbrüchen, die als Rohstoffquellen für Baumaterialien wie Beton und Gipskarton dienen. So hat die östlich gelegene Pabco-Gipsmine, die im James-Bond-Abenteuer *Diamonds Are Forever* (1971) gezeigt wurde, eine jährliche Kapazität von über 300.000 Quadratkilometern an Gipskartonplatten und sendet einen beständigen Strom von bis zu 200 großen LKW-Ladungen täglich über die geologische „Great Unconformity" zu Baustellen in Las Vegas und darüber hinaus. (S. 152 unten rechts) Auf dem Gebiet der westlich gelegenen James-Hardie-Mine (Blue Diamond) sollen 8400 hochpreisige Wohneinheiten entstehen. Dieser scheinbar effiziente Übergang von der Ausbeutung zur Nutzung als Bauland ist wegen der bedrohlichen Nähe der Mine zum Red-Rock-Canyon-Naturschutzgebiet jedoch sehr kontrovers.[36] Im Süden werden Kies und andere Zuschlagstoffe im Sloan-Steinbruch gefördert, der auf einer dominanten Anhöhe über den immer weiter vordringenden Häuserreihen aufragt. (S. 151, 167) Nach Norden hin schließlich gähnt eine weitere gewaltige Kiesgrube zwischen Lone Mountain und der Wildnis der Le Madre Mountains. Einst weit von der Stadt entfernt, wird sie rasch von den Wohnbauten mittlerer Größe eingeholt, die immer tiefer in die Seitentäler der Le Madre Mountains vordringen. Sind diese Steinbrüche auch nicht so eindrucksvoll wie die von Edward Burtynsky andernorts fotografierten, so sind sie in ihrer unmittelbaren Nähe zu den neuen Baugebieten doch frappierend.[37] (S. 152 oben und unten links) Ein solch direktes Nebeneinander von Ursprungsort und Endprodukt wirkt nachhaltig irritierend. Auf die perfekte Vision eines allumfassenden Spektakels konzentriert, verschließt Las Vegas die Augen vor diesen Kontrasten. Während visuelle Brüche, die mit den Urbanisierungsprozessen zusammenhängen, oft wortwörtlich durch aufgewirbelten Staub verschleiert werden, wird anhaltende Umweltzerstörung oft durch gute Absichten verdunkelt.

Auf unbehagliche Weise gehen in einer Umgebung stark beanspruchter Ressourcen Verbrauch und Verseuchung Hand in Hand, und die Narben der Umweltzerstörung werden durch die gewaltigen Distanzen der Mojave-Wüste verborgen. Zu den am stärksten verunstalteten und kontaminierten

Nevada Reno) estimates that "5% of abandoned mines cause some kind of environmental damage" and the Environmental Protection Agency (EPA) estimates that about "40% of watersheds in the western United States" are affected by mining pollution.[31]

As mineral wealth is supplanted by real estate wealth, the sites of extraction haunt contemporary urbanization in surprising ways. Nevada is home to between 225,000 and 310,000 abandoned mines, about 50,000 of which pose hazard to the general public through simple physical danger. In 1996 two bodies were found in an abandoned mine that, due to carbon dioxide pockets, was posted with the sign "Keep Out-Bad Air".[32] In 1999 a girl plummeted 180 feet down a shaft north of Las Vegas. Following this J. Davitt McAteer reported that "Nevada's past and present are bracing for a collision" and emphasized that suburban sprawl and abandoned sites of extraction are not easily compatible.[33] The area is particularly treacherous for those who practice rough-terrain sports such as biking and driving all-terrain vehicles that can easily plunge into deep, unfenced openings. In 2007 two young girls riding an all-terrain vehicle plummeted down a 125-foot shaft while following their father on a holiday weekend ride in the desert surrounding the small town of Chloride just east of Las Vegas, an unfortunate incident further underscoring such dangers.[34]

Other phenomena in the metropolitan area are of equal danger. Much of the muted brown Las Vegas Valley is characterized by disconcertingly bright green turf prized by Americans for their lawns and the image of suburban wholesomeness. Hoping to conserve water, new developments are now turning to "xeriscaping," a form of landscaping using only stone, gravel, and drought-resistant planting indigenous to the region. This is, unfortunately, not without risk and cases have arisen in which the stone and gravel used for xeriscaping were hauled from abandoned mines. Laden with sulfide minerals, such decorative landscaping stone poses the danger of heavy metal contamination through dust inhalation or touch, and yet further health hazards if such contaminants enter the city's water supply.[35]

Today the desert around the city is marked less by the search for precious chemicals or metals than by immense gravel and gypsum quarries, used as sources of raw materials for construction supplies such as concrete and wallboard. To the east, the Pabco gypsum mine can produce more than one billion square feet of wallboard annually. Featured in the James Bond adventure *Diamonds Are Forever* (1971), the mine can send a daily stream of up to 200 truckloads of wallboard over the geological "Great Unconformity" to construction sites in Las Vegas and beyond. (p. 152 bottom right) To the west, the James Hardie (Blue Diamond) gypsum

Orten gehören die Militärgebiete: Räume, „frei von Hindernissen oder Regulierungen", in denen die Army Unmengen von Munition verpulverte. Zu Beginn des Kalten Krieges begrüßten die Einwohner Nevadas die Aneignung von Land im Interesse von Patriotismus und ökonomischem Segen; die finanziellen Vorteile von Ausbeutung und Zerstörung ähneln sich. Doch die Erhabenheit der Wüste ist mit der über sie gebrachten gewaltsamen Zerstörung genauso schwer in Einklang zu bringen wie die Ausbeutung des Landes mit seiner Nutzung als Baugrund.

Richard Misrachs Fotografie zeigt wohl am deutlichsten die „Misshandlungen" der Mojave-Wüste durch den Menschen, um mit den Worten Reyner Banhams zu sprechen.[38] Wie Banham ist Misrach von van Dyke beeinflusst, er distanzierte sich jedoch von Bildern einer erhabenen Landschaft wie denjenigen von Ansel Adams, da sie einen „Mythos [aufrechterhalten], der Menschen davon abhält, die Wahrheit dessen zu sehen, was wir der Wildnis angetan haben".[39] Im Gegensatz zu Banham geht es ihm weniger um visuellen Genuss als vielmehr darum, „Zeugnis abzulegen".[40] Anne Wilkes Tucker schreibt, dass die Bilder von Richard Misrach „uns leicht davon überzeugen, dass unentwickeltes Wüstengelände großartig sein kann" und fügt hinzu, dass seine Fotografien „zerstörter Landstriche schwer mit dem Konzept der Schönheit zu versöhnen sind [...] wie kann man formale Schönheit mit Themen und Problemen in Verbindung bringen, die zu besorgniserregend sind, um mit Genuss verbunden zu werden"?[41]

Bravo 20: The Bombing of the American West und *Violent Legacies: Three Cantos* illustrieren am deutlichsten Misrachs Fähigkeit, solch schwerwiegende Themen in verstörenden Bildern von Gewalt und Verseuchung festzuhalten.[42] Die Totenschädel von Mustangs, wilden Pferden, die infolge verunreinigten Wassers neben militärischen Testgeländen starben, evozieren eine andere gewalttätige Szene in John Hustons *The Misfits* (1961), in der in Nevada Flugzeuge erbarmungslos Mustangs zusammentreiben, um sie zu fangen und zu töten. Und die Ausrottung wilder Tiere ist nicht nur auf eine ferne Vergangenheit beschränkt: 2007 verlangte Senator Harry Reid eine „‚vollständige und gründliche Aufklärung' der Tode von 71 wilden Pferden" auf dem Übungsgelände der United States Air Force in Tonopah, die auf Nitratverseuchung des Wassers zurückgeführt wurden:[43] Dies war eine Reaktion auf das „Massensterben" von 61 Pferden in derselben Gegend 1988 und auf Ängste, dass das Trinkwasser durch von der Air Force verwendete Enteisungsmittel verunreinigt sein könnte.[44]

Für unbefugte Personen unzugänglich, bleiben diese Gebiete dem Blick der Öffentlichkeit verborgen. Versteckte Landstriche wie Nevadas Area 51 – vor Ort bekannt als „Traumland" –, bleiben auf vielen Karten weiß, als

mine is proposed for conversion to a site for 8,400 units of upscale housing. A seemingly efficient transition from extraction to construction, it is highly controversial in its precipitous encroachment on the Red Rock Canyon conservation area.[36] To the south, gravel and other aggregates are being extracted from the Sloan quarry situated on a dominant hilltop looming over rows of encroaching housing below. (pp. 151, 167) Finally, to the north, yet another immense gravel quarry yawns between Lone Mountain and the Le Madre Mountain Wilderness. Once far removed from the city, mid-scale housing is rapidly overtaking the quarry even as it digs ever deeper into the flanks of the Le Madre Mountains. While these quarries aren't as formally impressive as those photographed elsewhere by Edward Burtynsky, they are striking in their immediate proximity to new developments.[37] (p. 152 top and bottom left) Such close juxtapositions of source and product often jar. Focused on a seamless vision of a totalizing spectacle, Las Vegas turns a blind eye towards contrasts that fit uneasily into a single frame of reference. While visual discontinuities associated with urbanization processes are often literally obscured by blowing dust, continuing environmental degradation is often obscured by good intentions.

Consumption and contamination coexist uneasily in an environment of quickly strained resources with the scars of environmental disruption concealed by the vast distances of the Mojave Desert. Military sites are among the most disrupted and contaminated sites: spaces "unhindered and unregulated" into which the military has hurled generations of munitions. At the inception of the Cold War, Nevadans welcomed the appropriation of federal land in the interests of patriotism and economic boon; the monetary benefits of extraction and destruction are not dissimilar. But the dichotomy of the desert sublime and the violent destruction visited upon it is as difficult to reconcile as the tension between extraction and construction.

Richard Misrach's photography is perhaps the best known for probing the tensions of, in the words of Reyner Banham, the "man-mauled" Mojave.[38] Like Banham, Misrach is influenced by van Dyke, but distances himself from images of a sublime landscape like those by Ansel Adams because they perpetuate a "myth that keeps people from looking at the truth about what we have done to the wilderness."[39] Unlike Banham, he is not concerned so much with visual pleasure, as with "bearing witness."[40] Anne Wilkes Tucker writes that Misrach's images "easily convince us that undeveloped desert terrain can be splendid," adding that nonetheless his photographs of "ravaged stretches of land are difficult to reconcile with the concept of beauty … how can one combine formal beauty with subjects and issues considered too grave to combine with pleasure?"[41]

sei Joseph Conrads *Herz der Finsternis* ins ausgedörrte Nevada versetzt worden. Aber die an diesen geheimen Orten stattfindenden Militärübungen haben ernste Auswirkungen auf die Struktur der Landschaft und ihre Bewohner. In *The Tainted Desert: Environmental and Social Ruin in the American West* beschreibt Valerie Kuletz, wie die Wüstenlandschaft durch 50 Jahre militärischer Experimente geformt, zerfurcht und zersplittert wurde; „Zeichen ihrer Macht sind Elektrozäune, Radarantennen, gewaltig zu den Sternen ausgerichtete Satellitenschüsseln, Überschallknalle, Stealthbomber, gut unterhaltene Straßen mitten im ‚Nirgendwo', die zu verschiedenen ‚Einrichtungen' führen […], Wachtürme, Absperrungen über Absperrungen und überall staatliche Schilder, auf denen ‚ZUTRITT VERBOTEN' zu lesen ist".[45]

Diese gewaltigen „Opferstätten" erstrecken sich von New Mexico bis Kalifornien: Bombenabwurf- und Artillerieschießplätze, nukleare Testgelände und stillgelegte Uranminen. Über 80 Prozent der Fläche Nevadas gehören dem Staat, der große Teile davon zu militärischen Zwecken nutzt. So liegt unweit nördlich von Las Vegas die Luftwaffenbasis Nellis. Ehemals wurde sie als Trainingsgebiet für Kriegseinsätze in Korea und Vietnam genutzt, aber die Wüstenumgebung ist besonders für die Simulation von Einsätzen im Mittleren Osten geeignet. Mit einer Fläche von ca. 8900 Quadratkilo-

metern, mehr als halb so groß wie der Bundesstaat Connecticut, umfasst Nellis auch das nukleare Testgelände Nevadas.[46] Hier wurden während des Kalten Krieges überirdische Nukleartests durchgeführt und die apokalyptische „Survival City" gebaut, um die Auswirkungen von Atomexplosionen auf Gebäude zu untersuchen. Wie Tom Vanderbilt schreibt, stellte „Survival City" die „Verkörperung aller Städte, ein architektonisches Stuntdouble der amerikanischen Lebensweise" dar.[47] Damals berichtete die *New York Times*, dass sich die Stadt „erstaunlich gut gegen den Schlag einer starken atomaren Detonation behauptete", den schwerwiegendsten Schaden erlitt die „Straße des Jüngsten Gerichtes".[48] Eine andere Explosion erschütterte Gebäude der 160 Kilometer entfernten Stadt Pioche, während der „Atompilz schnell bis auf eine Höhe von 35.000 Fuß aufstieg und ostwärts zog".[49] Während der Atomtests wurden Einwohner des südlichen Nevada und Utahs, die sogenannten „downwinders", mit Strahlungsmessern versorgt, um zufällige Bestrahlung zu überwachen. In einem Brief an „Menschen, die in der Nähe der Nevada Test Site leben" berichtete der Manager von Camp Mercury zuversichtlich, dass „manche von Euch gelegentlich möglichen Gefahren durch Blitz, Explosion oder Fallout ausgesetzt waren. Ihr habt die Unannehmlichkeit oder das Risiko ohne Umstände akzeptiert".[50] Ken Cooper beschreibt, wie die Atomic Energy Commission (AEC) in dieser Ära

Misrach's ability to capture such grave issues with disturbing images of violence and contamination are best illustrated in his *Bravo 20: The Bombing of the American West* and *Violent Legacies: Three Cantos*.[42] The death masks of mustangs, wild horses that died as a result of contamination near military test sites, echo another scene of violence from John Huston's *The Misfits* (1961), filmed in Nevada, in which aircraft mercilessly herd mustangs for capture and destruction. Eradicating wildlife through contamination is not consigned to a distant past: in 2007 Senator Harry Reid demanded a "'full and thorough investigation' into the [water-related] nitrate contamination deaths of 71 wild horses" at the United States Air Force's Tonopah Test Range.[43] This followed a "die-off" of 61 horses in the same area in 1988 and fears that drinking water might be contaminated by the de-icing compounds used by the Air Force.[44]

Off-limits to unauthorized personnel, military sites preclude ready public monitoring. Like an arid mirror of Joseph Conrad's *Heart of Darkness*, hidden landscapes such as Nevada's Area 51, locally known as "Dreamland," remain essentially blank on many maps. However, the effects of the military exercises taking place on these secretive sites profoundly impact the organization of the landscape and inhabitants throughout the region. In her *The Tainted Desert: Environmental and Social Ruin in the American West*, Valerie Kuletz describes the desert landscape as shaped, bifurcated and compartmentalized by fifty years of military experimentation, its signs of "power including high-wire fences, radar antennae, massive satellite communications dishes tilted up toward the stars, sonic booms, stealth aircraft, well-maintained roads in the middle of 'nowhere' leading to various 'installations' ... guard towers and, fencing and more fencing, and everywhere government signs that read 'DO NOT ENTER'."[45]

These are great "zones of sacrifice" stretching from New Mexico to California and they include bombing and artillery ranges, nuclear test sites and abandoned uranium mines. More than eighty percent of Nevada's land is owned by the federal government, and much of it is dedicated to military uses. Just north of Las Vegas lies the Nellis Air Force Range. Once used to as an area to train pilots for combat missions in Korea and Vietnam, the desert environment is particularly well suited for simulating missions in the Middle East. Comprising nearly 5,500 square miles, an area almost equal in size to the state of Connecticut, Nellis holds the (nuclear) Nevada Test Site.[46] Above ground nuclear testing was carried out here during the Cold War and the apocalyptic "Survival City" was built to study the effects of atomic explosions on buildings. As Tom Vanderbilt writes, it was the "embodiment of all towns, an architectural stunt-double for the American way of life."[47] At the

„atomaren Roulettes" „die öffentliche Meinung durch Filme, Broschüren und Schulvorführungen sorgsam kontrollierte".[51]

Heute hingegen löst die geplante Atommülldeponie am Yucca Mountain große Kontroversen aus. Kritiker protestieren vehement gegen die Realisierung des 1987 entwickelten Vorhabens. Solch große Gebiete, die, trümmer- und schuttbedeckt, als Lagerstätte für Atommüll dienen, erinnern uns daran, dass die Wüste in dem Glauben in Besitz genommen wurde, dass sie „wirklich für nichts anderes als einen Artillerieübungsplatz gut war – man konnte sie einem Bombenhagel aussetzen und niemand würde einen Unterschied wahrnehmen".[52] Das Resultat dieser Übungen ähnelt dem der Förderindustrien: eine oftmals radikale Umgestaltung der Wüste, kontaminiert und mit industriellem Schutt übersät. In Nevada allein umfassen diese „Spielplätze für das Militär" über 16 Millionen Quadratkilometer.[53]

Der Westen bietet nicht nur Spielplätze für das Militär und eine Heimat für Goldschürfer, Viehzüchter oder Visionäre. Neuerdings bietet er auch Raum für die Bedürfnisse des Freizeittourismus und der Lifestyle-Wirtschaft. Die Eisenbahn des 19. Jahrhunderts hatte einen „stählernen Weg durch die Wildnis" gebahnt und damit den Westen für den Tourismus erschlossen.[54] Am Ende des Jahrhunderts gaben steigender Wohlstand und ein neues Interesse an den Schönheiten der Natur der individuellen

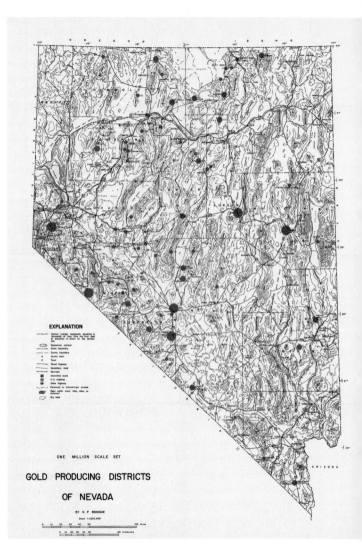

EXPLANATION

ONE MILLION SCALE SET

GOLD PRODUCING DISTRICTS

OF NEVADA

BY H. F. BONHAM

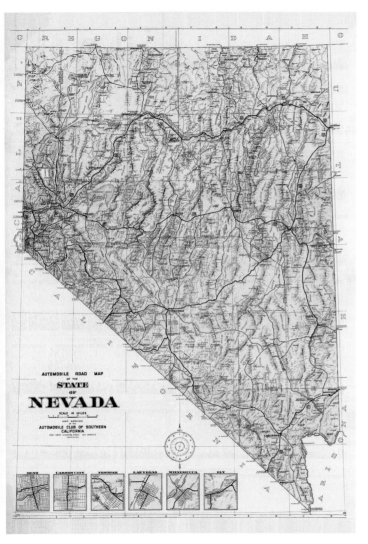

AUTOMOBILE ROAD MAP
OF THE
STATE
OF
NEVADA

SCALE IN MILES

MAP SERVICE
OF THE
AUTOMOBILE CLUB OF SOUTHERN
CALIFORNIA

time, the *New York Times* reported that it "stood up surprisingly well against the wallop of a big atomic blast" with the most serious damage occurring to the city's "Doomsday Drive."[48] Another blast vibrated buildings in the town of Pioche, 100 miles distant, while the "mushroom cloud rose rapidly to more than 35,000 feet and moved eastwards."[49] During the years of above-ground atomic testing, residents of southern Nevada and Utah were termed "downwinders" and given radiation badges to monitor accidental exposure to radiation. In a letter to "people who live near (the) Nevada Test Site," the test manager at Camp Mercury sanguinely reports that at "times some of you have been exposed to potential risk from flash, blast, or fall-out. You have accepted the inconvenience or the risk without fuss ...".[50] Ken Cooper describes this era of "atomic roulette" as one in which the Atomic Energy Commission (AEC) "carefully managed public opinion through films, brochures, and classroom demonstrations."[51]

The projected nuclear waste storage site at Yucca Mountain, chosen in 1987, is also a source of great controversy. Opponents argue vehemently against the realization of this plan. Such vast tracts covered in the detritus of destruction that serve as depositories for nuclear waste remind us that the desert was appropriated with the belief that it "really wasn't much good for anything but gunnery practice – you could bomb it into oblivion and

Mobilität Vorrang vor der kollektiven Erfahrung des Bahnreisens. Organisationen wie die League of American Wheelmen (für Radfahrer) und das Good Roads Movement halfen, neue Ziele zu erschließen.[55] Im frühen 20. Jahrhundert forderte das Schlagwort vom „Automobil auf dem Land" – eine Variation der „Maschine im Garten" (Leo Marx) – zur „Wiederentdeckung" Amerikas per Auto auf.[56] Auch die „See America First!"-Kampagne von 1906 sollte den Tourismus ankurbeln: Ihr Regionalismus war auch „eine Antwort auf die zentralisierenden Kräfte, die den entstehenden industriellen Nationalstaat umgestalteten" und berief sich dagegen auf ältere Traditionen des naturbezogenen „Monumentalismus" und des amerikanischen Exzeptionalismus.[57]

Solche Kampagnen hatten einen gewaltigen Einfluss auf den Bau von Straßen, die speziell für den Landschaftstourismus in den Wüsten des Westens geplant wurden. 1914 gab es in Kalifornien über 16.000 Kilometer befestigter Straße, in Nevada hingegen nur 421 Kilometer.[58] 1915 rollte der millionste Model-T-Ford vom Fließband, und 1921 wurde der „Federal Highway Act" verabschiedet, der ein Straßennetz für eine zunehmend mobile Öffentlichkeit vorsah.[59] Im Westen wurden die für den Landschaftstourismus gebauten Straßen bei der Schaffung von Nationalparks berücksichtigt. Auch wurde beabsichtigt, die reisende Öffentlichkeit, der vorherrschenden

protestantischen Arbeitsmoral entsprechend, dazu zu erziehen, nicht einfach „Reifengummi bei müßigen Urlaubsreisen zu verbrennen".[60]

Trotzdem opponierten Ortsansässige wiederholt gegen diese Art von „Spielplätzen für wohlhabende städtische Autofahrer" und wendeten ein, dass „Erholungsgebiete für Einwohner Nevadas für viele von uns ein Witz sind. Wir haben die ganze Umgebung, um uns zu erholen".[61] Trotz des Widerstandes wurden Pläne entwickelt, den Yosemite-Nationalpark mit dem bei Las Vegas gelegenen Valley of Fire, der Lost City, den Lehman-Höhlen und dem Zion-Nationalpark in Utah zu verbinden. Vorstöße zur Entwicklung eines bundesstaatlichen Parksystems verliefen jedoch im Sande: Aufgrund der konservativen Einstellung seiner Bürger und auch, weil es keine so spektakulären landschaftlichen Sehenswürdigkeiten wie Arizona oder Utah besaß, blieb Nevada im Hinblick auf Landschaftstourismus unterentwickelt. Man verließ sich auf „Scheidung, Heirat und Glücksspiel", um Besucher von außerhalb des Staates anzulocken.[62] In der Tat ist die Landschaft von Nevada weniger spektakulär und dadurch schwieriger „abzubilden" als die dramatischen Felsformationen und „Naturwunder" des Monument Valley, von Zion oder des Grand Canyon. Vielleicht sind nicht zuletzt aus diesem Grund die Reklametafeln hier besonders eindrucksvoll – die „Neon-Metropole" prägt jedenfalls in hohem Maße die landläufige Vorstellung von Nevada.

never notice the difference."[52] The end result of these exercises is similar to that of the extractive industries: an often radical reshaping of the desert, contaminated and littered with industrial debris. In Nevada alone, these "playgrounds for the military" amount to some four million acres.[53]

The west not only offers playgrounds to the military or a home to prospectors, cattlemen, and visionaries. It also accommodates the spatial organization and facilities of recreational tourism and the "lifestyle economy." The nineteenth century railroad thrust a "line of steel into the wilderness" and opened the west to tourism.[54] At the close of that century, increased wealth and a concern for natural aesthetics emphasized the freedom of personal mobility over the collective experience of rail travel. Exploration opportunities quickly developed with the support of organizations such as the League of American Wheelmen (for cyclists) and the Good Roads Movement.[55] The early twentieth century brought the notion of "the automobile in the country," a variation on the "machine in the garden," calling for the "re-discovery" of America by car.[56] This was paralleled in 1906 by the explicit boosterism of the "See America First" campaign, which promoted a sense of western regionalism in "response to the centralizing forces that were reconfiguring the emerging industrial nation-state" and underscored older traditions of natural "monumentalism" and American exceptionalism.[57]

Such campaigns had a tremendous impact on the construction of roads designed for scenic tourism in the desert west. In 1914, California had more than 10,000 miles of surfaced roads whereas Nevada had just 262.[58] However, 1915 saw the one millionth Model-T Ford roll off the assembly line, and, in 1921, a Federal Highway Act was passed to establish a network of roads for an increasingly mobilized public.[59] In the west, roads built for scenic tourism were closely aligned with the creation of state parks. This was also coupled with the intention of educating the traveling public to avoid conflict with the prevailing protestant work ethic by not simply "burn[ing] rubber in idle vacation travel."[60]

Nonetheless, locals often opposed these "playgrounds for well-to-do urban automobilists," and in Nevada it was argued that "recreation areas for Nevada people can not seem much other than a joke to many of us. We have the whole outside world to recreate in ...".[61] Despite such opposition plans were soon underway to link California's Yosemite National Park with Nevada's Valley of Fire and Lost City, both near Las Vegas, and to Lehman Caves and Zion National Park to the east. Tentative steps were taken to develop a state park system, but with a locally conservative political constituency and a lack of the monumental landscapes of Arizona and Utah, Nevada was left a scenic-tourism backwater, relying on "divorce, marriage, and gambling"

Der Autobahn-Tourismus, ob er nun floriert wie in Kalifornien, Utah und Arizona oder eher stagniert wie in Nevada, beruht auf dem visuellen Konsum von Landschaft. Erst in der Nachkriegszeit löste jedoch das Aufkommen von Offroad-Aktivitäten einen bedeutenden Umschwung vom Landschafts- zum Erlebnistourismus aus. Geländefahrzeuge, wie Jeeps, Dünenfahrzeuge, Motorräder, Motorschlitten und Jetboote gehören zu den wichtigsten Formen mechanisierter Freizeitaktivitäten. Dazu kommt eine Flut an Mountainbikern, Ski- und Kajakfahrern sowie Kletterern, die dem nicht-mechanisierten Freizeiterlebnis frönen. Die Landschaft vor den Folgen von „zuviel Freizeit" zu schützen, ist daher kein einfaches Unterfangen.

So verlieh beispielsweise der „Wilderness Act" von 1964 dem staatlichen Bureau of Land Management (BLM) die Befugnis, Landstriche als „Wildnis" zu deklarieren, als Gebiet, „in dem die Erde und ihre Lebensgemeinschaft vom Menschen unbehindert ist, in dem der Mensch ein Besucher ist, der nicht bleibt."[63] Vorübergehende Nutzung kann jedoch genauso schädlich wie permanente Beanspruchung sein. So alarmierte 1976 Science News die Öffentlichkeit über die Auswirkungen des jährlichen Motorradrennens durch die Mojave-Wüste, das vom kalifornischen Barstow über 240 Kilometer nach Las Vegas führte. Es wurde geschätzt, dass durch das Rennen bis zu diesem Zeitpunkt nahezu 36.500

Quadratkilometer Wüstenland samt Flora und Fauna sowie archäologische Stätten zerstört worden waren.[64] Zwar wurde das Rennen aufgegeben, doch der beträchtliche Bevölkerungszuwachs und die steigende Anzahl von Geländewagen in den Wüsten des Westens setzen die geschützte Landschaft zunehmend unter Druck. Heute wird angenommen, dass mehr als 28 Millionen Eigenheime weniger als „30 Meilen von in Bundesbesitz befindlichem Land [entfernt sind], das Millionen von Menschen als ihren erweiterten Garten ansehen."[65] Motorenlärm und Abgase verschärfen das Problem; zudem ist der Zugang zu öffentlichem oftmals nur über privates Land möglich, was von dessen Besitzern nicht gern gesehen wird.

Das Geschäft mit der Offroad-Erholung floriert derart, dass heute sogar Stadtmarketing-Firmen auf dieser Welle schwimmen. So entwickelten R&R Partners, die Agentur hinter der „Only in Vegas"-Marketingkampagne, 2003 eine „Nevada Passage Adventure Competition", um Nevadas Entertainmentangebot zu erweitern. Dieser als Realityshow konzipierte Wettbewerb präsentierte das ländliche Nevada als erstklassiges Ziel für Abenteuerurlaub. Zwanzig Kandidaten maßen sich quer durch den Bundesstaat im Klettern, Jetbootfahren, Geländefahren, Mountainbiking, Sandboarding und Kajakfahren.[66] Kritiker beschrieben diese Verwandlung des Alten Westens in den neuen Freizeit-Westen als Schaffung eines

tourism as the primary focus for out-of-state visitors.[62] Indeed, lacking in the dramatic rock formations and natural wonders of Monument Valley, Zion, or the Grand Canyon, Nevada's less spectacular scenery is difficult to "image." Nevada's spectacular signage reflects this, as does the degree to which the "neon metropolis" now frames the image of the state in the popular imagination.

Scenic highway tourism, whether flourishing in California, Utah and Arizona, or languishing in Nevada, focuses on a visual consumption of the landscape. But it was the postwar era and the advent of the off-road activities that brought with them a major shift in emphasis from scenic tourism to recreational tourism. Off-road vehicles (ORVs) or all-terrain vehicles (ATVs) like de-militarized jeeps, dune buggies, motorcycles, snowmobiles, and jet skis, are the primary forms of mechanized recreation. Today, an explosion in mountain biking, skiing, kayaking, rock climbing and other forms of non-mechanized recreation must be added to this list. Protecting lands from the effects of "over-recreation" is a difficult and contested undertaking.

The Wilderness Act of 1964, for example, granted the federal Bureau of Land Management (BLM) the authority to set aside lands as wilderness, defined as "area[s] where the earth and its community of life are untrammeled by man, where man himself is a visitor who does not remain."[63] But transient usage can be just as harmful as permanent occupation. In 1976 *Science News* raised the alarm about the "Fragile Desert" with regard to the annual 150-mile Barstow (California) to Las Vegas motorbike race across the Mojave. It was determined that the race had destroyed more than 9000 acres of desert, with plant and animal life, as well as archaeological sites.[64] Since discontinued, substantial population increases combined with rapidly increasing numbers of ATVs throughout the desert west have nonetheless put ever-new pressures on protected lands. Today it is estimated that "more than 28 million homes" are located "less than 30 miles from federally owned land that millions of people increasingly view as their extended backyards."[65] Engine noise and emissions add to the problem, as do issues of accessing public lands through private lands whose owners may wish to resist such transgressions.

Off-road recreation is a booming business and today even urban marketing firms are riding this trend. Seeking to diversify Nevada's entertainment profile, R&R Partners, the firm behind the "Only in Vegas" advertising campaign, developed "The Nevada Passage Adventure Competition" in 2003. This reality-show competition showcased rural Nevada as a premier destination for outdoor adventure travel in which twenty individuals were selected to participate in a competition including

„Themenparks" oder einer „Urlaubskolonie" für wirtschaftlich Privilegierte.[67] Falls dieses Argument richtig ist, wie die Kampagne von R&R Partners nahelegen könnte, dann hat es keinen Sinn mehr, Las Vegas und die Mojave-Wüste jeweils unterschiedlichen Themenbereichen zuzuordnen. Die grundlegenden Unterschiede zwischen Stadt und Wüste, die in der Gegenüberstellung der Schriften Venturis und Scott Browns mit denen Banhams so evident sind, wären damit eingeebnet. Es steht also zu erwarten, dass der Slogan „What plays in the Mojave, stays in the Mojave" die erhabene Ödnis und Leere der Wüste in eine Freizeit-Utopie verwandeln wird, übersät von Golfplätzen und von den Reifenspuren der Geländewagen durchkreuzt.

Demgegenüber argumentiert jedoch Kerwin Klein, dass Unterscheidungen immer erhalten bleiben werden, dass die Grenzen von „Parks, Monumenten, Wildnisgebieten und Wäldern" einen „radikalen Unterschied" zwischen den „'unentwickelten' Räumen auf der anderen Seite der *Frontier*, dem Exotisch-Anderen, und den entwickelten Stadtlandschaften des modernen Amerika" markieren.[68] Für Klein stellen die noch vorhandenen räumlichen Grenzen eine „Wahrnehmungsschwelle zu den scheinbar unstrukturierten Räumen des öffentlichen Landes dar", die weiterhin in deutlichem Gegensatz zu der „strukturierten alltäglichen Welt" stehen.[69] Die kinematografische Darstellung des Westens hat dazu beigetragen,

diese Wahrnehmungsschwelle zu verfestigen; die Landschaft selbst trägt den „fantastischen Eindruck dieser Bilder [in sich], gespenstische Spuren ihrer Gegenwart erfüllen die großartigen leeren Räume […]".[70] Es ist ein interessantes Argument, dass die Wüste – egal, wie gründlich sie in ein Freizeit-Wunderland verwandelt werden mag – für immer eine Grenze in Form eines „Wüstenimaginären" darstellen wird; eines Imaginären, das, wie Edward Buscombe bemerkte, größtenteils in Hollywood kreiert wurde.[71]

Anders als in Hollywood ist es jedoch nicht möglich, „Cut" zu rufen, um eine Szene durch eine andere zu ersetzen und Helden und Komparsen Seite an Seite dem Sonnenuntergang und einem neuen Kampf entgegenreiten zu lassen. Ob an den Orten der Ausbeutung, Militarisierung oder Freizeit, die Veränderungen der Landschaft sind real, sie bieten sich eher für die postapokalyptischen Bilder von *Mad Max 2: The Road Warrior* [um einmal eine Anleihe bei der australischen Wüste zu machen] an als für John Fords Western oder die Roadmovies Dennis Hoppers, Richard Sarafians oder Ridley Scotts.[72] Klein unterstreicht die Bedeutung von Bildern für die Konstruktion der Landschaft des Westens, auch wenn diese Bildwelten für ihn die „Gegen-Bilder" eines Richard Misrach noch nicht enthalten. In gleicher Weise ist, wie wir gesehen haben, dieser „scheinbar unstrukturierte Raum" schon höchst strukturiert und enthält vielfältige Orte des Übergangs.

rock climbing, jet skiing, off-road driving, mountain biking, sandboarding and kayaking across the state.[66] Critics have described such transformations of the old west into the new recreational west as the creation of a "theme park" or "leisure colony" for the economically privileged.[67] If this argument is correct, as R&R Partners' campaign might underscore, then the theming of Las Vegas and the theming of the Mojave have been elided. This erases the fundamental distinctions between the two so evident in the writings of Venturi and Scott Brown as contrasted with those of Banham. Thus we may anticipate the slogan "What plays in the Mojave, stays in the Mojave," and the final transformation of the desert from the sublimity of the vast and empty into a recreational utopia dotted with golf courses and crisscrossed by ATV tracks.

On the other hand, Kerwin Klein argues that distinctions will remain because the boundaries of "parks, monuments, wilderness areas, and forests" are reified as a mark of "radical difference" between the "'undeveloped' spaces on the far side of the frontier constitut(ing) an exotic other, contrasting sharply with the developed urban landscapes of modern America."[68] In Klein's view, extant spatial boundaries constitute a "perceptual threshold into the seemingly unstructured space of the public lands" that continue to exist in sharp contrast to the "structured workaday world."[69] The reification of this perceptual threshold has been underscored by the cinematic representation of the west, the western landscape itself retaining the "imaginative impress of these images, ghostly traces of their passage filling the great empty spaces…".[70] It is an interesting argument, that no matter how great the transformation of the desert into a recreational wonderland might be, it will forever remain frontier in the form of a "desert imaginary;" an imaginary largely created, as Edward Buscombe discusses, in Hollywood.[71]

Unlike Hollywood, however, it is not possible to yell "cut," replacing one scene with another, and letting heroes and extras alike ride into the sunset to fight another day. Whether in the sites of extraction, militarization or recreation, the changes to the physical landscape are real, lending themselves more readily to the post-apocalyptic images of *Mad Max 2: The Road Warrior*, to borrow from the Australian desert, than to John Ford's westerns or the road movies of Dennis Hopper, Richard Sarafian, or Ridley Scott.[72] What Klein does underscore is the importance of imagery in constructing the landscape of the west even if, for Klein, this imagery does not yet include the "counter-images" of a Richard Misrach. Similarly, as we have seen, this "seemingly unstructured space" is already highly structured, containing within it multiple sites in transition.

Das Abbilden des dritten Ortes

Die komplexe historische und räumliche Matrix der Mojave ist von Dichotomien, Divisionen und Kollisionen gezeichnet: Wüste und Stadt, Form und Raum, Zeichen und Symbol, Erfolg und Scheitern, Struktur und Chaos. *Die Urbanisierung der Mojave-Wüste: Las Vegas* stellt diese starren Einteilungen infrage und fokussiert stattdessen die über diese Dualismen hinausführenden Bewegungen und die Zwischenräume, die durch diese Oszillationen gebildet werden. Statt Dualismen von Natur und Kultur oder getrennte Orte der Ausbeutung, Militarisierung und Erholung abzubilden, sehen wir diese Räume als hybride Orte, die durch die wechselseitigen Verunreinigungen zwischen physischen und kulturellen Geografien geprägt sind. Sie sind „alltägliche" Orte, die durch die komplexen Beziehungen zwischen Praktiken der Produktion und des Konsums, lokalen und globalen Akteuren, sowie physischen und virtuellen Räumen erzeugt werden. Erneut werden auch Fragen nach der fotografischen Darstellung der äußerst komplexen Wüstenumgebung aufgeworfen.

Auf den vorangehenden Seiten erwähnten wir Darstellungen des natürlichen Erhabenen von Watkins und Adams, die Unterwerfung dieses Erhabenen in den Bergbaufotografien O'Sullivans und Henry Jacksons und die Verseuchung durch die Hinterlassenschaften des nuklearen Erhabenen, wie Misrach sie einfing. Außerdem sprachen wir Lynchs „View from the Road" sowie Scott Browns, Ruschas und Shores Bilder alltäglicher Budenarchitektur an. Ein wichtiger zeitgenössischer Fotograf ist Mark Klett, Klett, der von der Ausstellung „New Topographics" (1975) beeinflusst ist wurde durch seine Serie von „Einst und Jetzt"-Fotografien bekannt.[73] Seir Blick auf diese Umgebung und seine Fotos, die die Veränderungen in der Landschaft sichtbar machen, hatten großen Einfluss auf die Entstehung der hier gezeigten Abbildungen. Keineswegs aber wollten wir damit Vergleiche zwischen verschiedenen Epochen oder unterschiedlichen Nutzungen der Wüste anstellen. Vielmehr wollten wir zeigen, wie sich Zeiten und Nutzungsweisen überschneiden und überlagern: Bilder sich verschiebender Identitäten und Orte zeitlichen und räumlichen Übergangs. In diesem Sinn können unsere Fotografien als *split screens*, als Mehrfach-, oder Kristallbilder gesehen werden, die die Vergangenheit aufgezeichneter Ereignisse mit der Gegenwart ihres Sehens verschmelzen. Sie bieten dritte Sichtweisen an, die die Orte des Übergangs als Orte im Übergang darstellen indem sie zwischen den Schichten der Geschichte und Erinnerung, der physischen und wahrgenommenen Zeit fluktuieren.

Diese Identitätsverschiebungen und hybriden Orte können auch im Kontext der differenzierten Schattierungen postkolonialer Kritik verstanden werden, indem sie Licht auf die komplexen Bedeutungen von „Eroberung

Imaging the Third Site

Dichotomies, divisions, and collisions characterize the Mojave's complex historical and spatial matrix: desert and city, form and space, sign and symbol, success and failure, structured and unstructured. *Urbanizing the Mojave Desert: Las Vegas* questions these fixed dualisms, focusing instead on the movement back and forth across these dualisms and the transitional sites created by such oscillations. Rather than imaging dualisms of nature and culture, or separate sites of extraction, militarization, and recreation, we see these as hybrid sites shaped by the mutual contamination of physical and cultural geographies. They are "everyday" sites created through the complex relations of production and consumption processes, local and global players, physical and virtual realms. We will interweave this discussion with issues of the photographic representation of this increasingly complex desert environment.

In the preceding pages we touched upon depictions of the natural sublime by Watkins and Adams, the subjugation of the natural sublime in the mining photography of O'Sullivan and Henry Jackson, the contamination of the natural sublime with the debris of the nuclear sublime as captured by Misrach. We have also touched on Lynch's "View from the Road" and images of the roadside vernacular by Scott Brown, Ruscha and Shore. An important contemporary photographer is Mark Klett. Influenced by the "New Topographics" exhibit (1975), Klett is well-recognized for his series of "then and now" photographs of the west, capturing aspects of its transitions.[73] These helped frame our understanding of the images presented here. Our intentions, however, were not to present contrasting times or uses, but overlapping and simultaneous ones: images of shifting identities and sites in transition. As such, our photographs can be seen as split screens or crystal images, confusing and fusing the pastness of recorded events with the presentness of their viewing. They offer third sights, framing the sites of transition as sights in transition, fluctuating between layers of history and memory, as well as physical and perceptual time.

Identity shifts and hybrid sites can also be understood within the differentiated shadings of postcolonial criticism. They reflect the complex meanings of "conquest" and "culture," the manner in which these meanings frame our understanding of the landscape and its inhabitants, as well as the manner in which Las Vegas accepts, manipulates, and challenges master discourses traditionally held dear by Americans. Against dominant tropes of American exceptionalism, Las Vegas insists on its own exceptional place.

Corresponding to ways in which postcolonial scholars challenge the reconstruction of local cultures through "western" discourses, historians of the "new west" hold Frederick Jackson Turner in a special and maligned

und „Kultur" werfen, darauf, wie diese Bedeutungen unser Verständnis der Landschaft und ihrer Bewohner bedingen und wie Las Vegas Diskurse, die den Amerikanern lieb und teuer sind, akzeptiert, manipuliert oder anficht. Entgegen der vielzitierten Vorstellung eines amerikanischen Exzeptionalismus besteht Las Vegas auf seiner eigenen herausragenden Rolle.

So, wie Vertreter der Postcolonial Studies die Konstruktion lokaler Kulturen durch „westliche" Diskurse hinterfragen, kritisieren Historiker des „neuen Westens" Frederick Jackson Turner für seine eurozentrische Sicht der Kolonisierung des Westens und für seine Überzeugung, nach der die amerikanische „Grenzerfahrung" den Charakter und die Entwicklung der Nation geformt habe.[74] In den letzten Jahrzehnten warfen Patricia Limerick und andere Historiker Turner vor, dass er „reale Orte des Westens nur als Bühnenbilder für sein unaufhörlich wiederholtes ‚Grenz-Drama'" behandle.[75] Anstatt die Geschichte des amerikanischen Westens als Geschichte einer Grenzverschiebung zu schreiben, plädiert Limerick dafür, den Westen als „realen Ort, als eine Region von Bedeutung mit einer ernstzunehmenden Geschichte" anzuerkennen.[76] Dies hieße, seine Geschichte neu zu schreiben, nicht als Widerstreit von „Grenze" und „Region" oder „Natur" und „Kultur", sondern im Hinblick auf ein detailliertes Verständnis der Begründung, Erfindung und Erschaffung des Westens. Eine solche Geschichte würde auch eine Untersuchung des „sense of place" einschließen,[77] wie er durch bislang von der Geschichtsschreibung ausgeschlossene Gruppen generiert wurde.[78] Will man die Geschichte(n) dieser „eher hybriden als reinen" Landschaften des Westens schreiben, muss man auch die Vorstellungen einer „unproblematischen" Natur hinterfragen, denen so viele Umweltschützer anhängen, und die komplexen Beziehungen zwischen Natur und Kultur erforschen.[79]

Darüberhinaus wurde dazu aufgerufen, internationalen Verbindungen mehr Aufmerksamkeit zu schenken und einen globaleren, vergleichenden Standpunkt einzunehmen, der den Fokus von der traditionellen Beziehung zwischen dem Osten und Westen Amerikas zu der globalen Beziehung zwischen Norden und Süden verschiebt.[80] Dies veränderte die Sicht auf die Metropolregion Las Vegas. Während Las Vegas von den 1930ern bis in die 70er-Jahre als „Erholungsort im ‚Sun Belt'" galt,[81] wurde die Stadt in jüngster Zeit als das „letzte Detroit" beschrieben, ein Schlagwort, das die Erlebnisindustrie der Stadt in den Kontext wirtschaftlichen Niedergangs im „Rust Belt" stellt.[82] Nach Patricia Ventura belegt dies die „Synthese zweier scheinbarer Antithesen: [Las Vegas] ist der neue Sun Belt und das neue Detroit".[83] Ventura sieht diese Synthese als Produkt der Globalisierung. Tatsächlich spiegelt der Strip von Las Vegas die Auflösung nationaler Grenzen und die Wirkung von Abkommen wie dem North American Free

place for his Eurocentric views on the colonization of the west and his arguments that the frontier experience shaped American character and development.[74] In recent decades, Patricia Limerick and other historians have criticized Tuner's thesis for treating "actual western places only as stage settings for the repeated sequential performances of the frontier play."[75] Instead of writing the history of the American west in terms of a shifting frontier, Limerick argues for recognizing "the American west as a real place, as a region of significance with a serious history."[76] Such a history would include the rewriting of the dichotomies of frontier versus region or nature versus culture in terms of a detailed understanding of the West's regional promotion, creation, and construction,[77] and an examination of the sense of place generated by groups previously excluded from writings of history.[78] In this regard, it is important to reexamine notions of an unproblematic nature held by many environmentalists, and to explore the complex relations between nature and culture with the goal of developing histories of "hybrid rather than pure landscapes" of the west.[79]

There has also been a call for increased attention to be paid to international connectivity, to adopt a more global, comparative approach that shifts the focus from the traditional relationship between America's east and west, to the global relationship of north and south.[80] This has altered perspectives on the Las Vegas metropolitan region. Whereas from the 1930s to the 1970s Las Vegas was seen as a "resort city in the sunbelt,"[81] it has recently been portrayed as the "last Detroit" with the city's experience economy framed in terms of rustbelt industries.[82] To Patricia Ventura, this argues for the "synthesis of two seeming antitheses: it is the New Sunbelt and the New Detroit."[83] For Ventura this synthesis is a product of globalization. Treatises such as the North American Free Trade Agreement (NAFTA) and the liquidation of national boundaries are enacted both "figuratively in the case of the Strip's worldwide themes and literally in the composition of its union workforce."[84] But while globalization benefits some in Las Vegas, the low wages characteristic beyond the Strip reflect disparities characterizing regions worldwide.

This network of relations between east and west, north and south, contrasts sharply with the inclusivist enthusiasm expressed by Venturi and Scott Brown. Social disparities are often obscured by the overriding manner in which Las Vegas has challenged dominant mores and spatial structures. Drawing on a seemingly endless supply of hydroelectric power from Hoover Dam, Las Vegas transformed Enlightenment culture into a culture of illumination constructed of ephemera: a city in which "if you take the signs away there is no place."[85] From its origins in the exotic desert casinos of

Trade Agreement (NAFTA) unmittelbar wider: „bildlich in [seinen] globalen Themenwelten und wortwörtlich in der internationalen Zusammensetzung seiner gewerkschaftlich organisierten Arbeiter".[84] Doch während die Globalisierung so manchen in Las Vegas zugute kommt, reflektieren die jenseits des Strip gezahlten Niedriglöhne die Ungleichheit, die so viele Orte auf der ganzen Welt kennzeichnet.

Dieses Netz von Beziehungen zwischen Osten und Westen, Norden und Süden steht in scharfem Kontrast zu der inklusivistischen Begeisterung, mit der Venturi und Scott Brown die Geburt eines neuen Urbanismus begrüßten. Und tatsächlich: die Art, in der Las Vegas herrschende Vorstellungen von Moral und (räumlicher) Ordnung herausforderte, verschleiert zunächst soziale Ungleichheiten. Der Hoover-Staudamm liefert die endlosen Megawatt Strom, mit deren Hilfe Las Vegas das Licht der Aufklärung in eine Kultur der Beleuchtung verwandelt hat, gebildet aus Nichtigkeiten: eine Stadt, in der „der Ort verschwindet, sobald man die Schilder entfernt".[85] Seit seinen Anfängen in den exotischen Wüstenkasinos der 40er- und 50er-Jahre ermöglichte das „suburbane Xanadu" „den Amerikanern, das Glücksspiel zugleich räumlich und kulturell unter Kontrolle zu halten".[86] Als Ort „ungesunder Verlockung" waren der Strip und die von ihm erzeugten Formen der Urbanisierung so kontrovers wie die von

ihnen beherbergten sozialen Aktivitäten.[87] In den Vereinigten Staaten hatte Nevada von 1931 bis 1978 ein „geografisches Monopol" für das Glücksspiel. Dieses Monopol brachte die Sorge um soziale Probleme wie die „ständige Fluktuation in der Arbeiterschaft" sowie „politische Korruption, das Eindringen organisierten Verbrechens, zwanghaftes Spielen, [...] Prostitution und Kreditwucher" mit sich.[88] Somit verkörperte das suburbane Xanadu weniger ein inklusivistisches Ideal als ein janusköpfiges „Doppel", eine gespaltene Identität, die von Natur aus flüchtig und instabil zwischen sittlich und widerlich, Unterhaltung und Ausbeutung oszillierte.

Räumliche Begrenzung war nötig, um diese Flüchtigkeit lange genug zu stabilisieren, dass finanzieller Gewinn durch Spiel und Unterhaltung möglich wurde. Wie David Schwartz bemerkte, sind Kasino-Resorts nicht insular, um Kunden vor äußerer Bedrohung zu schützen, sondern um sie „drinnen zu halten [...], sie sind keine Festungen, sondern Gefängnisse".[89] Mittlerweile hat der goldene Käfig die Form luxuriöser Wohntürme auf mehrgeschossigen Parkhäusern angenommen, die den Wohnraum vom öffentlichen Raum isolieren und so eine vertikale Variation der vielen Gated Communities darstellen, die die Stadt umgeben. Diese Orte der Separation, Kontrolle und Gefangenschaft verkörpern eine räumliche Strategie des „Architainment", eine fiktionale Erzählung europäischer und asiatischer

1940s and 1950s, the "suburban Xanadu" permitted "Americans to contain gambling in both space and culture."[86] A place of "unwholesome allure," the Strip and the forms of urbanization it engendered have been as controversial as the social activities they housed.[87] Within the United States, Nevada had a "geographic monopoly" on gambling from 1931 until 1978, a monopoly that carried with it concern for social problems such as a "highly transient workforce" as well as "political corruption, organized crime infiltration, compulsive gambling ... prostitution and loan sharking."[88] Thus the suburban Xanadu embodied less an inclusivist ideal than a Janus-faced "double" or divided identity; an identity that was inherently fluid and unstable as it moved between wholesome and loathsome, entertainment and exploitation.

Stabilizing such fluidity for periods long enough to guarantee financial gain from gaming and entertainment, required spatial confinement. As David Schwartz has noted, casino resorts are insular. This is not to protect patrons from external threat, but to "keep their patrons inside ... they are not fortresses but prisons."[89] Today the gilded cage has been extended to the development of luxury residential towers set atop multi-story car parks, isolating residential from public space in a vertical variation on the many gated communities encircling the city. These sites of separation, control and confinement embody the spatial strategy of "architainment," blending a fictional narration of European or Asian places with hidden exits, dim lighting, and blissful humming; a crossbreed that Norman Klein calls "happy imprisonment" or the "labyrinth effect."[90]

Transforming the broad vistas of the desert sublime into labyrinthian spatial regimes produces an environment of camouflage and concealment not aligned with contemporary concerns for surveillance and control. Thus, in an odd twist, "America's playground" also serves as its "security lab." Shifting identities has prompted Las Vegas to serve as an incubator for a host of surveillance technologies seeking answers to "who are you?", a questioning title and refrain used as the musical theme for *CSI: Crime Scene Investigation*.[91] Enormously successful, *CSI* portrays forensic police probing criminal cases with the latest technologies in order to discover the "true" identities of victims and perpetrators. Questions of identity are also asked by casino operators using "eye in the sky" surveillance technology to evaluate suspicious gambling behavior associated with cheating. Such surveillance includes facial recognition programs sharing information throughout casino networks as well as radio frequency identification (RFID) chips embedded in casino chips enabling wager amounts on roulette numbers or baccarat spots to be tracked. The national security industries are also asking "who

Orte, gebildet durch versteckte Ausgänge, abgedunkeltes Licht und das selige Brummen der Maschinen; diese Kreuzung bezeichnet Norman Klein als „glückliche Gefangenschaft" oder „Labyrinth-Effekt".[90]

Die weite Aussicht auf die Erhabenheit der Wüste wurde eingetauscht gegen labyrinthische Ordnungssysteme; daraus erwächst ein Umfeld der Tarnung und Verheimlichung, das mit den zeitgenössischen Bedenken gegenüber Überwachung und Kontrolle in Widerspruch steht. Durch eine seltsame Umwidmung dient „Amerikas Spielplatz" zugleich als sein „Labor für Sicherheit". Las Vegas ist zum Brutkasten für zahlreiche Überwachungstechnologien geworden; „Who are you?", fragt der Titelsong der Fernsehserie *CSI: Crime Scene Investigation*.[91] Mit großem Erfolg porträtiert *CSI* die Untersuchungen forensischer Fahnder, die mit den neuesten Technologien die „wahren" Identitäten der Opfer und Täter von Kriminalfällen festzustellen suchen. Fragen nach der Identität stellen auch die Kasinobetreiber, die „Eye in the Sky"-Überwachungstechnologien dazu verwenden, das Verhalten der Spieler auf Anzeichen von Betrug auszuwerten. Über vernetzte Gesichtserkennungsprogramme tauschen die Kasinos Informationen aus, Funksender in Spielchips erlauben es, Wettbeträge auf Roulettenummern oder Baccaratpunkte zu verfolgen. Auch die nationalen Sicherheitsindustrien fragen „Wer bist Du?" und

verwenden von der Kasinoindustrie entwickelte Technologien in ihrem Kampf gegen den Terrorismus.[92]

Die Frage nach der eigenen Identität wird jedoch selten von der Stadt selbst gestellt. Bilder der Stadt reproduzieren Muster fröhlicher überschäumender Marketingkampagnen. In seiner Studie *Beautiful Children* erinnert uns der in Las Vegas geborene Charles Bock daran, dass eines der ersten Mega-Resort-Kasinos, das MGM Grand, in das smaragdgrüne Licht des *Wizard of Oz* getaucht ist, des berühmtesten Films der MGM-Studios.[93] Las Vegas, die Smaragd-Stadt für den Mittelstand Amerikas, wuchs heran zu einer Stadt der Vagabunden und Gauner; ein gigantischer Schwindel in Gestalt einer Stadt, die ihre Identität an Markttrends und Fantasiegebilder ausrichtete – von Bugsy Siegel zu Walt Disney. Aber die Forderungen nach Beständigkeit wuchsen und aus der Verwandlungskünstlerin wurde eines der „stärksten städtischen Modelle im Amerika des 20. Jahrhunderts".[94] Galt sie einst als Anomalie, so betrachten sie einige nun als Prototyp einer „All-American City".[95] Aus der Sicht von Urbanisten unterstreicht Las Vegas mit dem das Straßenraster schnurgerade durchschneidenden Strip den Paradigmenwechsel von monozentrischen Modellen der Urbanisierung zu einer „polyzentrischen Metropole allgegenwärtigen, scheinbar grenzenlosen, parzellierten Sprawls".[96] Einst nicht mehr als ein Haltepunkt der

are you?". In pursuit of counterterrorism initiatives they test technologies developed by the casino industry.[92]

This question of "who are you?", however, is seldom asked of the city itself. Images of the city replicate a pattern of joyful and exuberant marketing campaigns. In his recent *Beautiful Children,* Las Vegas-born Charles Bock reminds us that the MGM Grand, one of the first of the mega-resort casinos, is bathed in the emerald green light of MGM´s most famous film, the *Wizard of Oz.*[93] As the Emerald City for much of middle-class America, Las Vegas came of age as a city of drifters and grifters; an urban confidence game shifting its identity in response to market trends and fantasy projections from Bugsy to Disney. But with ever-increasing claims to permanence, this shape-shifter has now been elevated to one of the "most potent urban models in twentieth-century America."[94] Once an anomaly, it is considered by some to be a prototype of an "All-American City."[95] With the linear Strip slicing an urban grid, urbanists see Las Vegas as underscoring the paradigm shift from monocentric models of urbanization to the "polycentric metropolis of ubiquitous, apparently limitless, parcelized sprawl" associated with Los Angeles.[96] Starting as a railroad stop and desert outpost, the city later described as the "first spectacle of the post-modern world" has transformed into the "center of the postindustrial world" in which the "old

pariah has become a paradigm, the colony of everywhere, the colonizer of its former masters."[97]

For Hal Rothman, Las Vegas came to "symbolize the new America," an icon unique in its ability to "attract and repel," a "mecca of postliterate faith" in which entertainment serves as culture.[98] Developing from colony to colonizer, the city importing everything from everywhere is now exporting this everywhere to anywhere. And a great deal of it is headed to China, where Las Vegas's casinos have been transplanted to the territory of Macau and the "Cotai Strip," an Asian mirror of the Las Vegas Strip. This "Strip versus Strip" simulation of simulacra raises the financial stakes in resort development, underscores the shifting character of global economics, and again destabilizes the place and image of Las Vegas.[99] The Venetian Macau, opened in 2007 at a cost of 2.4 billion dollars, is the "largest single-structure hotel in Asia and the second largest building in the world" according to its parent company, the Las Vegas Sands.[100] Drawing throngs of visitors, the company hopes to invest up to twelve billion dollars in constructing twenty thousand hotels rooms by 2010. Other additions to the Cotai Strip originating in Las Vegas include the Wynn Macao and the MGM Grand Macau,[101] respectively opened in 2006 and late 2007.[102] The globalization of Disneyland has been superseded by the globalization of the Strip and in

Eisenbahn und Vorposten in der Wüste, verwandelte sich die später als „erstes Spektakel der postmodernen Welt" beschriebene Stadt in ein „Zentrum der postindustriellen Welt", in der der „alte Paria zum Paradigma, die Kolonie von Überall zur Kolonisatorin ihrer früheren Herren wurde".[97]

Nach Hal Rothman entwickelte sich Las Vegas zu einem „Symbol des neuen Amerika", zu einem einzigartigen Sinnbild der Anziehung und Abstoßung, dem „Mekka einer postliteraten Religion", dem Unterhaltung als Kultur dient.[98] Die Stadt, die alles von überall her importierte, exportiert dieses Allerorts nun überall hin, sie entwickelt sich von der Kolonie zum Kolonisator. Vieles davon geht nach China, wo die Kasinos von Las Vegas in das Territorium Macaos und des „Cotai Strip", eines asiatischen Spiegels des Las Vegas Strip, transplantiert wurden. Diese „Strip versus Strip" Simulation der Simulacra erhöht die finanziellen Einsätze in der Entwicklung von Resorts, unterstreicht den beweglichen Charakter globaler Ökonomie und destabilisiert den Ort und das Bild von Las Vegas.[99] Das Venetian Macau, 2007 für 2,4 Milliarden Dollar gebaut, ist nach Aussagen der Muttergesellschaft Las Vegas Sands das „größte Hotel Asiens und das zweitgrößte Gebäude der Welt".[100] Aufgrund der hohen Besucherzahlen hofft die Gesellschaft bis 2010 rund zwölf Milliarden Dollar in den Bau von 20.000 Hotelzimmern zu investieren. Das 2006 eröffnete Wynn Macao und das 2007 eingeweihte MGM Grand Macau[101] sind weitere von Las Vegas ausgehende Projekte des Cotai Strip.[102] 2007 wählte das britische Konsortium International Leisure Development einen Ort in der Wüste Spaniens für einen neuen Las-Vegas-Klon – „Gran Escala" – aus: Die Globalisierung Disneylands wurde von der des Strip überholt.[103]

Wurde Las Vegas, als Modell und durch ihr Vermögen, zur „Kolonisatorin ihrer ehemaligen Herren", so wird die Gefälligkeit nun durch solvente Investoren erwidert, die nach zu erobernden Märkten suchen. Die frühe Grenze der westlichen Zwischengebirge entwickelte sich in einem Klima, in dem „Eroberung und städtische Expansion sich in die Hände spielten".[104] Heute entspricht das von Las Vegas in auswärtigen Resorts angelegte Kapital fremden Kapitalanlagen in Las Vegas, die einige der größten und angesehensten Projekte des Valleys absichern. Dubai World, das durch politischen Druck dazu aufgefordert wurde, sich aus den Holdings der Häfen von New York bis New Orleans zurückzuziehen, investierte viel in das neue Las Vegas. Die Gesellschaft beteiligte sich mit fünf Milliarden Dollar an MGM Mirage und ist gleichberechtigter Partner in dem 308 Quadratkilometer großen CityCenter-Projekt, das mit seiner Lage am Strip mit sieben Milliarden Dollar veranschlagt wird.[105] Mit solchen Projekten hat sich Las Vegas von der Stadt der Flüchtigkeit zur Metropole des Monumentalen

2007 the British consortium International Leisure Development chose the deserts of Spain for yet another "Gran Escala" Vegas redux.[103]

If Las Vegas, as a model and with its wealth, has become the "colonizer of its former masters," the favor is reciprocated by investors flush with funds and looking for new markets to conquer. The early frontier of the intermountain west evolved in a climate in which "conquest and urban expansion fed each other."[104] Today, investments by Las Vegas in foreign resort industries are mirrored by foreign investments in Las Vegas underwriting some of the largest and most prestigious projects in the valley. Dubai World, prompted by political pressure to divest itself of American port holdings from New York to New Orleans, has invested heavily in the new Las Vegas. It has infused an estimated five billion dollars in MGM Mirage and secured equal partnership in the 76-acre CityCenter project located along the Strip and valued at more than seven billion dollars.[105]

With such projects, Las Vegas has evolved from the ephemeral to the monumental while continuing to present itself as a site of the temporal exception: the momentary transformation into an alter-ego or the desired Other in terms of "what plays ... stays." But physical development is also accompanied by the double of virtual marketing and projections to other times, places and spaces. Featuring a seductive soundtrack, CityCenter's website advertises itself simply as "Into the New." Asking virtual visitors to "take a walk through the future of urban living" the project moves "from a dream to a city." The latter could be a quote from Sony Picture's *Bugsy*, the film mythologizing Las Vegas's founding by New York gangster Bugsy Siegel as easily as it could be from MGM's *Wizard of Oz*. Located between the older New York New York and the new, "urban-themed" Cosmopolitan, CityCenter also signals the entry of global architectural players into the Las Vegas market, once dominated by locals. The marketing campaign lauds the new "masterminds" Norman Foster, Rafael Vinoly, Helmut Jahn, Daniel Libeskind, and Kohn, Pederson, Fox.[106] As financial reserves flow from oil-rich enclaves and architectural talent flows from a global pool, China supplies industrial goods ranging from structural steel to sophisticated curtain wall systems.

On the northern end of the Strip, on the site of the former New Frontier, another transformation is taking place. The Israeli-based Elad Group, responsible for the luxury conversion of New York's Plaza Hotel, purchased a 36-acre property and is creating the five-billion dollar Las Vegas Plaza, scheduled to open in 2012. As the "manhattanization" of the Las Vegas Strip advances, major investments are continuing along the periphery of the valley, appropriating federal land under the Southern Nevada Public Land Management Act of 1998. Instructing the Bureau of Land Manage-

entwickelt, während sie sich zugleich als Ort zeitlicher Ausnahme präsentiert: die zeitweilige Transformation in ein Alter Ego oder das ersehnte Andersartige im Sinne von „what plays ... stays". Diese materielle Entwicklung geht jedoch auch mit virtueller Vermarktung und den Projektionen in andere Zeiten, Orte und Räume einher. Mit verführerischem Soundtrack bewirbt die Website von CityCenter das Projekt einfach mit „Into the New". Das Projekt verwandelt sich „von einem Traum in eine Stadt", indem es virtuelle Besucher dazu auffordert „durch die Zukunft urbanen Lebens zu spazieren". Das erstere könnte ein Zitat aus *Bugsy* (Sony Pictures) sein, einem Film, der die Gründung von Las Vegas durch den New Yorker Gangster Bugsy Siegel als ein Kinderspiel darstellt. Mit seiner Lage zwischen dem älteren New York New York und dem neuen, „urban ausgerichteten" Cosmopolitan signalisiert das CityCenter auch die Ankunft der Global Player auf dem Architekturmarkt von Las Vegas, der zuvor von lokalen Firmen beherrscht wurde. So preist die Marketingkampagne Norman Foster, Rafael Vinoly, Helmut Jahn, Daniel Libeskind und Kohn, Pederson, Fox als die neuen „Köpfe" an.[106] Während Finanzmittel aus ölreichen Enklaven und architektonisches Talent aus einem globalen Pool fließen, werden die für den Bau der Projekte verwendeten industriellen Güter vom Baustahl bis zu hochentwickelten Vorhangfassaden aus China geliefert.

Am Nordende des Strip, am Ort des ehemaligen New Frontier, findet eine andere Verwandlung statt. Hier kaufte die in Israel ansässige Elad Group, die für die luxuriöse Konversion von New Yorks Plaza Hotel verantwortlich ist, eine 146 Quadratkilometer große Liegenschaft und baut das fünf Milliarden Dollar teure Las Vegas Plaza, das 2012 eröffnen soll. In dem Maß, in dem die „Manhattanisierung" des Las Vegas Strip fortschreitet, setzen sich bedeutende Investitionen entlang der Peripherie des Valley fort, für die bundeseigenes Land nach dem Nevada Public Land Management Act von 1998 verkauft wird. Das Bureau of Land Management ist angewiesen, 218,5 Hektar zu versteigern (2002 auf 307,5 Hektar erweitert), nach jüngsten Schätzungen wird dieser Vorrat innerhalb von sechs Jahren erschöpft sein.[107] Entlang des südlichen Talrandes transformiert der aus Hongkong stammende Projektentwickler und Vorsitzende von New World China Land, Henry Cheng Kar-shun, die Konturen des Vegas Valley mit dem 2,6 Hektar großen Crystal Ridge Projekt, das über dem luxuriösen Roma Hills Development aus den McCullough Mountains herausgeschnitten wird.[108] (S. 156, 160, 161, 171)

In einer Gegend, die für ihre große Zahl an Speed- („crystal amphetamine") Konsumenten bekannt ist, formt das hochkarätige Crystal-Ridge-Projekt ohne Sinn für die Ironie des Unternehmens die Höhenlinien des

ehemaligen Bundesgebietes radikal um. Dabei geht man ähnlich vor wie bei den Grundstücksentwicklungen im Kalifornien der 50er-Jahre, als beim berüchtigten „mountain-topping" mittels Sprengladungen von bis zu 60.000 Pfund das Gelände für 472 Eigenheime eingeebnet wurde.[109] [S. 156] Im Hinblick auf die verursachten Umweltschäden kann sich dieses Bauprojekt damit ohne weiteres mit den traditionellen Förderindustrien messen. Etablierte amerikanische Firmen wie Del Webb, Pardee und KB Homes steuern einen großen Teil der lokalen Planung mit großmaßstäblichen und spektakulären Projekten, wie dem am südöstlichen Rand des Valley gelegenen Lake Las Vegas. Hier wurde auf 14 Hektar ehemaligen Bundeslandes ein von 3000 Wohneinheiten umgebener künstlicher See angelegt, ein Dorf im mediterranen Stil mit einem eigenen „Ponte Vecchio" und venezianischen Gondeln. [S. 9, 170, 172] Angesichts finanzieller Schwierigkeiten während der Immobilienkrise von 2007–2008 wendeten sich die Entwickler an koreanische und schweizerische Käufer, um die Kredite tilgen zu können.[110]

Die Verflechtung von Las Vegas' realen und kinematografischen Räumen veranlasste den Stadtgeografen Michael Dear zu der Folgerung, dass die Architektur des Strip ein wahrhaftes Medienprodukt ist, das „sich am Kino orientiert. Die Hotels sind Filmbauten und Tonstudios, in die normale Leute kommen, um zu leben, zu spielen und Rollen anzunehmen."[111] Nach Norman Klein orientieren sich die Resorts von Las Vegas international, indem sie „Tourismus, Einzelhandel und Kino in einem bisher unmöglichen Maßstab verbinden."[112] Das Resultat dieser Orientierung ist ein „scripted space", ein geschriebener Raum illusionistischer Effekte, der Erfahrungen hervorruft, die denen von Videospielen, Themenparks und vor allem des Kinos ähneln.[113] War dieses „scripting" einst auf die Fantasiekreationen des Strip beschränkt, so dehnt es sich zunehmend auf die unzähligen Lifestyle-Gemeinden an und jenseits der städtischen Peripherie aus. [S. 170, 171]

Diese Verbindung der realen und kinematografischen Stadt ermöglicht es, gleichzeitig eine sonnige Vergangenheit und eine düstere Zukunft heraufzubeschwören. Während *Viva Las Vegas!* (1964), Elvis Presleys kokettes Gerangel mit Ann-Margret, eine Stadttour enthielt, die sich von einer ironischen Schießerei im Last Frontier Village zu einem Helikopterflug über den Lake Mead erstreckte, wirft uns Russell Mulcahys *Resident Evil Extinction* (2007) in einen brutalen Kampf mit unnachgiebigen Zombies über der sandgefüllten Lagune des Kasinos Venetian. Als düstere dystopische Vision zeigt *Extinction* eine der Wüste ausgelieferte Stadt.

Vor mehr als 20 Jahren erinnerte uns Marc Reisner an die Blütezeiten und den Verfall bedeutender Wüstenzivilisationen und wies darauf hin, dass im amerikanischen Westen „was Wasser betrifft, Logik und

ment to auction 54,000 acres (expanded to 76,000 acres in 2002), recent predictions claim that this land might be exhausted within six years.[107] Along the city's southern edge the Hong Kong developer Henry Cheng Kar-shun, Chairman of New World China Land, is transforming the physical contours of the Las Vegas Valley with Crystal Ridge, a 642-acre project carved out of the McCullough Mountains above the luxury development of Roma Hills.[108] (pp. 156, 160, 161, 171)

With no sense of irony in a region known for its heavy users of crystal amphetamine, the high-end Crystal Ridge development is reshaping mountain ridgelines of what used to be federal land in a manner akin to the "mountain-topping" practices decried in mid-century California developments. (p. 56) Explosive charges of up to 60,000 pounds have been used to level sites for the 472 private-home sites.[109] As such, this development competes with the environmental impact engendered by traditional extractive industries. Large-scale developments by established American corporations like Del Webb, Pardee, and KB Homes drive much local planning as well as spectacles of development, such as Lake Las Vegas at the extreme southeastern edge of the valley. Here, on 3,500 acres complete with a 320-acre man-made lake surrounded by 3000 residential units, a "Mediterranean-style" village with its own "Ponte Vecchio" and Venetian gondolas has been created on what had been federal land. (pp. 9, 170, 172) In financial difficulty during the housing downturn of 2007–2008, the development turned to Korean and Swiss buyers to meet credit payments.[110]

Las Vegas also interweaves physical and virtual spaces, leading urban geographer Michael Dear to conclude that the architecture of the Strip is truly a media product taking "its lead quite literally from the movies. The hotels are film sets and sound stages on which ordinary people come to live, play, and act out."[111] Norman Klein asserts that Las Vegas' resorts orient themselves internationally by, "linking tourism, retail sales and cinema on a scale never possible before."[112] The result of this orientation is a "scripted space," consisting of illusionistic effects evoking experiences resembling those of video games, theme park rides and, most particularly, the cinema.[113] If this scripting was once limited to the fantasy creations of the Strip, it is increasingly extended to the many "lifestyle" communities at the city's periphery and beyond. (pp. 170, 171)

The linkage of real and reel also allows for simultaneous presentations of a sunny past and a dark future. Whereas Elvis Presley's flirtatious romp with Ann-Margret in *Viva Las Vegas!* (1964) featured a city tour ranging from a tongue-in-cheek gunfight at the Last Frontier Village to a helicopter ride over a burgeoning Lake Mead, Russell Mulcahy's *Resident Evil: Extinction* (2007)

Verstand in der Planung nie eine bedeutende Rolle gespielt haben".[114] Heute führen zunehmende Trockenheit auf der einen Seite, ständig steigender Wasserbedarf auf der anderen Seite dazu, dass der Lake Mead immer hemmungsloser angezapft wird; laut Schätzungen von Experten des Scripps Institute of Oceanography könnte der See 2021 ausgetrocknet sein.[115] (S. 74) Trotzdem werden am Lake Las Vegas noch immer üppige italienische Gärten und Golfplätze über die Wüstenhügel drapiert. Damit diese Fata Morgana mitten in der Wüste erscheinen konnte, musste der Las Vegas Wash, einst ein natürliches und ökologisch empfindliches Wasserverteilungssystem, in zwei Rohren von rund 2,44 Metern Durchmesser kanalisiert und unter dem Lake Las Vegas hindurch dem schwindenden Lake Mead zugeführt werden. (S. 172, 185)

50 Meilen nördlich von Las Vegas wurde in einem abgelegenen Gebiet, das einst als Raketentestgelände hatte dienen sollen, mit dem Bau des Coyote Springs Resorts begonnen: geplant sind 150.000 Wohneinheiten, „geschäftiges Straßenleben", 15 Golfplätze, Seen und Wasserlandschaften auf 174 Hektar.[116] (S. 189) Zwar sind Maßnahmen wie Xeriscaping vorgesehen, doch das Projekt dreht sich vorwiegend um Golf, Wassersport und unklare „Lifestyle"-Aktivitäten. Coyote Springs wird sich ausgedehnte Wasserressourcen aneignen, um diese Freizeitaktivitäten zu sichern. Es

wird möglicherweise Tierschutzgebiete trockenlegen und dadurch zum Gegenstand von Klagen durch Umweltschützer werden.[117] Wie an vielen Orten in der Mojave handelt es sich bei diesem umfassenden Zugriff auf die begrenzten Wasservorräte tatsächlich um eine Art Abbau von und Raubbau an Rohstoffreserven, um eine Industrie, die nicht so sehr elementare Bedürfnisse als vielmehr fragwürdige Sehnsüchte bedient.

In der Erfüllung solcher Sehnsüchte tritt eine Einstellung zutage, die sich am deutlichsten im Wasserverbrauch von Las Vegas spiegelt: in der Negation der Wüste.[118] Las Vegas wird über eine Vielzahl von über- und unterirdischen Quellen mit Wasser versorgt, die sichtbarsten sind der Colorado River und die Reservoirs entlang seines Laufes. Lake Mead wird von Lake Powell, Lake Mojave und Lake Havasu eingefasst, die alle durch den Colorado River und seine Nebenarme versorgt werden. Insgesamt haben sieben Bundesstaaten und Mexiko Rechte auf das Wasser des Colorado, die prozentuale Verteilung wird durch komplexe Richtlinien bestimmt, die spezifische Menge hängt vom Wasserstand ab, der an Lees Ferry in Arizona gemessen wird.[119] Die Einwohner von Las Vegas sind stolz darauf, die nationale Wachstumsliste anzuführen, was sich in den 660 Litern Wasser widerspiegelt, die hier täglich pro Kopf verbraucht werden. Im Gesamtsystem erhöht sich der Pro-Kopf-Verbrauch auf schwindel

features a brutal fight with unyielding zombies over the sand-filled lagoon of the Venetian Casino. A bleakly dystopian vision, *Extinction* pictures a Las Vegas utterly abandoned to the desert.

More than twenty years ago Marc Reisner reminded us of the great desert civilizations that flourished and then collapsed, suggesting that in the American west "where water is concerned, logic and reason have never figured prominently in the scheme of things."[114] Today Lake Mead is being rapidly depleted as drought intersects ever-increasing demand and researchers at the Scripps Institute of Oceanography have projected that Lake Mead may go dry by the year 2021.[115] (p. 74) Nonetheless, at Lake Las Vegas, lush Italian garden terraces and golf courses continue to be draped over desert hillsides. Creating such a desert mirage required submerging the Las Vegas Wash, a once natural and ecologically sensitive drainage system, confining the limited water to two 96-inch diameter pipes flowing under Lake Las Vegas towards the dwindling Lake Mead. (pp. 172, 185)

At Coyote Springs, fifty miles north of Las Vegas in an isolated area once reserved as a rocket test site, a new development project envisioning 150,000 residences, "buzzing village streetscapes," 15 golf courses, lakes, and water parks covering 43,000 acres has started construction.[116] (p. 189) Despite introducing measures such as xeriscaping, these creations

evolve, and revolve, around golf, boating, and vague "lifestyle" activities. Coyote Springs will appropriate extensive water resources, potentially draining wildlife sanctuaries to supply recreational entertainment, making it the object of litigation by environmental groups.[117] As with many sites in the Mojave Desert, accessing limited water resources for such vast interventions can be understood as an extractive industry, one serving not only vital needs but questionable desires.

Fulfilling such desires exhibits what some term "desert denial," an attitude reflected most clearly in the city's water consumption.[118] Water is supplied by a variety of sources from both above and below ground; the most visible of these are the Colorado River and the reservoirs along its course. Lake Mead is bracketed by Lake Powell, Lake Mojave and Lake Havasu, which are all fed by the Colorado River and its tributaries. Altogether, seven states and Mexico have rights to the waters of the Colorado, the percentages determined by complex apportionment guidelines and adjusted according to the flow of water measured at Lee's Ferry, Arizona.[119] Las Vegans pride themselves on being at the top of the nation's growth lists, and, at 660 liters per day, their per capita water consumption mirrors this. System wide, daily per capita consumption climbs to a staggering 971 liters per day.[120] The Colorado River's limited resources have triggered the search for additional

erregende 971 Liter täglich.[120] Die Ressourcen des Colorado sind begrenzt und man versucht, neue Quellen zu erschließen, unter anderem einen regionalen Grundwasserspeicher, der sich von Salt Lake City in Utah bis zum Death Valley in Kalifornien erstreckt. Daraus ließen sich jährlich fast 250 Millionen Kubikmeter Wasser gewinnen, die Folge wäre jedoch zugleich das Absinken des Grundwassers in mindestens 78 Becken über fast 130 Hektar und damit eine schwere Beeinträchtigung des bereits fragilen Ökosystems. Das Absinken des Wasserspiegels der Quellen, Feuchtgebiete und Wasserläufe würde die Existenz von 20 bundesweit geschützten und 137 weiteren einheimischen Tierarten sowie von Tausenden ländlicher Haushalte und Landwirtschaftsbetriebe in der Region bedrohen.[121] Trotzdem planen die Wasserbehörden Süd-Nevadas, die Ressourcen des Nordens zu nutzen, um Las Vegas mit dem Wasser zu versorgen, das die Stadt für ihr Wachstum zu benötigen glaubt. Dieser Plan wurde kürzlich mit dem historischen Wasserdiebstahl im Owens Valley in Kalifornien verglichen.[122]

Solche Prozesse der Umwandlung stellen die Wahrnehmung der Wüste als „exotisches Andersartiges" weiter infrage und legen einen Begriff des Exotischen nahe, der eher mit denjenigen Prozessen der Globalisierung verbunden ist, die Distanz und Unterschiedlichkeit auslöschen.[123] In diesem Sinn argumentiert der Literaturwissenschaftler Ackbar Abbas, dass ein solches Exotisches eine „Fremdheit [betone], die keine Entfremdung hervorruft".[124] Es ist eher ein Hybrid, ein „Chiasmus" oder eine Kreuzung zwischen dem Fremden und dem Vertrauten, der einen Ort nicht im Hinblick auf seine Verschiedenheit von einem anderen betrachtet, sondern im Hinblick darauf, „wie fremd oder fern er sich selbst ist".[125] In Coyote Springs zeigt sich dieses Exotische in einer Marketingkampagne, die den Ort als „Golfplatz-Gemeinde" ankündigt, die „auf der leeren Leinwand der Wüste zu erträumen" sei.[126] Dem Gestalter des Golfplatzes zufolge ist dieses „Wüstenmeisterwerk" „durch die Berge im Hintergrund inspiriert und ahmt diese nach", es generiert eine Landschaft in „verbessertem Wüstenstil"[127] und garantiert einen „sorglosen Golfplatz-Lifestyle".[128] Der Golfplatz als Doppelgänger der Wüste ist nicht der einzige unheimliche Aspekt des Projektes. Nach dem Vorbild verschiedener „Signature-" Golfplätze gestaltet, wird Coyote Springs im Golftourismus als „Weltklasse"-Reiseziel vermarktet.[129] [S. 187, 189]

Zunehmend richtet sich die Strategie von „Golfplatz-Gemeinden" und innerstädtischen Entwicklungsprojekten an ein globales Publikum. Die neueren Kasinos betonen die „Manhattanisierung" des Strip, und Projekte wie das *Cosmopolitan* und das *CityCenter* unterstreichen den internationalen Charakter der Stadt. Diese Entwicklung setzt verstärkt auf die Geschwindigkeit

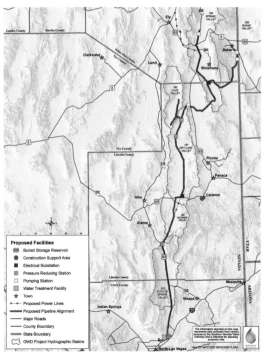

sources of water. These include a regional groundwater aquifer extending from Salt Lake City, Utah, to Death Valley, California. Accessing this aquifer would provide almost 250 million cubic meters of water annually. It would also cause groundwater levels to drop across at least 78 basins over nearly 130,000 square kilometers, greatly impacting a fragile ecosystem. Drops in the water table, spring discharge, wetland area, and streamflow would adversely affect 20 federally listed species, 137 other water-dependent endemic species, as well as thousands of rural domestic and agricultural water users in the region.[121] Nonetheless, Southern Nevada Water authorities plan to use the aquifers of Northern Nevada to supply Las Vegas with the water it needs for its profligate growth, a plan recently compared with the historic Owens Valley water grab in California.[122]

Such processes of conversion further challenge the notion of the desert as an "exotic other," suggesting a notion of the exotic as associated with the processes of globalization that erase distance and difference.[123] The literary critic Ackbar Abbas argues that such exoticism stresses "strangeness that does not produce estrangement."[124] Rather, it serves as a hybrid, a "chiasmus" or crossover between the foreign and the familiar that frames one place not in terms of its difference from another but in terms of "how [it] is different or distanced from itself."[125] Thus, at Coyote

und die Wirkung von Bildern. Wie die „leere Leinwand der Wüste" wird die Stadt zu einem Bildschirm für „die Sprache des Spektakels und den Exotismus des Neuen".[130] Diesen Raum visueller Sättigung bezeichnet Abbas als „Raum des schon Verschwundenen".[131] Aufbauend auf Henri Lefebvres Kritik eines neokapitalistischen „abstrakten Raumes" charakterisiert er diesen Raum als „(negative) Erfahrung einer unsichtbaren Ordnung der Dinge", einer Ordnung, die er die „zeitgenössische Form des Kolonialen" nennt.[132]

Hal Rothman sieht eine solche ökonomische und räumliche Ordnung in Las Vegas realisiert. Er bezeichnet den Tourismus als die „kolonialistischste aller kolonialen Ökonomien, nicht wegen der physischen Schwere oder der Qual und der Demütigung, die der Arbeit innewohnt, sondern als Resultat der psychischen und sozialen Auswirkungen auf Völker und ihre Orte".[133] In Las Vegas zeigen sich die unterschiedlichen Facetten dieses Kolonialismus wie auf einem *split screen*, um im kinematografischen Bild zu bleiben: Die Stadt ist ein Kaleidoskop von Orten des psychologischen Eskapismus, der physischen Regeneration und der städtischen Rekreation. Die Stadt erfindet sich beständig neu, nirgends sind urbane Identitäten „flüchtiger, transitorischer, weniger begründet auf irgendetwas anderes als menschlicher Einbildungskraft".[134] Die ständigen Identitätswechsel sind zugleich Produkt und Produzent der Ökonomie des Tourismus. Obwohl als saubere Industrie angesehen, ist der Tourismus Teil der modernen, postindustriellen und postmodernen Welten und „seine sozialen Strukturen und kulturellen Wege sind die einer Förderindustrie".[135] Rothman sieht Las Vegas wie andere Zentren der Massenproduktion als Ort eines „industriellen Tourismus", hier wird das Erlebnis zur Ware und die Umwelt nach den jeweils neuesten Trends und Erwartungen verpackt.[136] Für ihn sind die Landschaften der Stadt von den „neurotischen, krampfhaften Bestrebungen, Wünsche zu industrialisieren" gezeichnet, sie resultieren aus einer mechanischen Reproduktion ihres Bildes, aus einem „kinematografischen Tourismus", der Nachbarschaften und Wüstenlandschaften in malerische Kulissen oder die Schwärze des Offscreen verwandelt.[137] Wie sich die Landschaften industrialisierten Begehrens, exotischen Dekors und umweltbezogener Schäden überlagern, wird besonders in Resorts wie Lake Las Vegas und Coyote Springs sowie in den elitären Enklaven von Roma Hills oder Crystal Ridge deutlich. Hier sind die Orte der Ausbeutung und des Aufbaus untrennbar mit denen der Abstraktion verbunden, die Besuchern und Besitzern ein komplexes Set bebilderter und eingebildeter Erlebnisse bieten.

Als wir das Projekt *Die Urbanisierung der Mojave-Wüste: Las Vegas* vor etwas mehr als zwei Jahren begannen, konnten wir uns noch nicht

Springs, the exotic is reflected in a marketing campaign announcing it as "golf course community" to be "imagine[d on] a blank desert canvas."[126] According to the golf course designer, this "desert masterpiece" is "inspired by and almost mimics the mountains in the backdrop," generating a landscape in an "enhanced desert style"[127] and ensuring a "carefree golf course lifestyle."[128] As a desert *Doppelgänger*, the golf course exhibits an uncanny side, but not its only one. Modeled after numerous "signature" golf courses, it is also marketed as a member of a specialized group of "world class" destinations.[129] (pp. 187, 189)

Targeting global audiences is an increasingly characteristic strategy of golf course communities and inner city developments. Casinos stress the "manhattanization" of the Strip and projects like the *Cosmopolitan* and *CityCenter* emphasize the international character of the city. This development wagers heavily on the speed and impact of images. Like the "blank desert canvas," the city becomes a screen for the "language of spectacle and the exoticism of the new."[130] Abbas calls this space of visual saturation the "space of the *déjà disparu*."[131] Building on Henri Lefebvre's critique of neocapitalist "abstract space", Abbas characterizes this space as the "(negative) experience of an invisible order of things," an order that he calls the "contemporary form of the colonial."[132]

Returning such an economic and spatial order to Las Vegas, Hal Rothman identifies tourism as the "most colonial of colonial economies, not because of the sheer physical difficulty or the pain or humiliation intrinsic to its labor, but as a result of its psychic and social impact on people and their places."[133] Las Vegas presents a multifaceted image, a split screen of sites of psychological escapism, physical regeneration, and urban recreation. The city constantly reinvents itself, creating an environment in which urban identities are nowhere "more fleeting, more transitory, less based in anything than the human imagination."[134] This continual shedding of identity produces, and is largely produced by, the tourist economy. Despite its reputation as a clean industry, tourism is part of the modern, postindustrial, and postmodern worlds and "its social structures and cultural ways are those of an extractive industry."[135] Like other centers serving a mass market, Las Vegas is portrayed as a site of "industrial tourism" characterized by the packaging of experience as a commodity and the reshaping of the environment in accordance with the latest trends and expectations.[136] The city's landscapes are marked by "neurotic struggles to industrialize desire," resulting in the mechanical reproduction of its image, in a "cinematic tourism" converting neighborhoods and desert environments into picturesque backdrops or a blackness offscreen.[137] The imbrication of

vorstellen, wie radikal sich das Las Vegas Valley in diesem kurzen Zeitraum verändern würde. Der kommerzielle Sektor war stark, der riesige Anbau des Venetian, „Palazzo", wurde eröffnet und die Touristenzahlen erreichten 2007 einen Rekord von 39,2 Millionen.[138] Trotz dieser Rekorde entließ MGM kürzlich 440 Manager.[139] Allerdings hat sich in den größeren Gebieten der Urbanisierung der Wüste die Stimmung dramatisch geändert. 2006 hallte Baustellenlärm über das Tal und Baustaub erfüllte die Luft. 2007 ging der Verkauf von Neubauten um fast 46 Prozent zurück, viele Baustellen liegen brach, die Bulldozer sind geparkt und die Bauarbeiter gegangen.[140] Der Hauptbauunternehmer von Lake Las Vegas blieb fällige Zahlungen von 500 Millionen Dollar schuldig und das Projekt ging in den Besitz eines von Credit Suisse geleiteten Anlagenkonsortiums über.[141] Die spektakuläre Eröffnung von Coyote Springs wurde verschoben. Das neueste Bild der Stadt ist von Schildern geprägt, die Zwangsvollstreckung ankündigen, und Busreisen bieten solventen Interessenten Touren trauriger Grundstücksverkäufe: Im gesamten Tal steht 7000 Eigenheimen die Zwangsvollstreckung bevor.[142] In den ersten Monaten von 2008 waren mehr Zwangsvollstreckungen als Verkäufe zu verzeichnen.[143] In vielerlei Hinsicht reflektiert Las Vegas nun die Geschichte zweier Städte. Die Geschichte könnte zu guter Letzt die Stadt eingeholt haben, die ihren Blick immer nur auf das Neue gerichtet hat.

Wir haben auf unseren Reisen durch das Las Vegas Valley und die Mojave-Wüste gelernt, dass Tal und Wüste zu viele Perspektiven und Einblicke bieten, um als *ein* Modell zu dienen oder in einfachen Kategorien bewertet werden zu können. Las Vegas entwickelte sich von einer westlichen Wüstenoase zu der „amerikanischen" Stadt Venturis und Scott Browns und dehnte sich – auch durch die Nord-Süd-Migration – zu der globalen Stadt aus, die sie heute ist. Nach der Rückkehr von unseren Reisen durch die realen, kinematografischen und literarischen Topografien – als modernistische Gegenwelt einer erhabenen Jenseitigkeit, als postmodernes Pastiche einer prototypisch-amerikanischen Alltäglichkeit und als postkoloniale hybride Landschaften, die durch Prozesse der Ausbeutung, Abstraktion, Militarisierung und Rekreation geformt sind – wurden die Fragen nach Erfolg und Scheitern der Urbanisierung in einer extremen und fragilen Umwelt dringender. Wichtige Antworten liegen in der Vorstellung, Abbildung und Deutung dieser komplexen und dynamischen Orte des Übergangs.

landscapes of industrial desire, exotic decorum, and environmental damage becomes particularly clear in resort developments such as Lake Las Vegas and Coyote Springs, as well as in elite enclaves such as Roma Hills or Crystal Ridge. Here, the sites of extraction and construction are fundamentally linked to those of abstraction, offering the visitor or owner a complex set of imaged and imagined experiences.

As we began the *Urbanizing the Mojave Desert: Las Vegas* project a little more than two years ago it would have been difficult to imagine the changes that have impacted the Las Vegas Valley in the short time since then. The commercial sector remains impressive, the huge "Palazzo" extension to the Venetian has opened, and tourist numbers reached a record 39.2 million in 2007.[138] Despite such strength, MGM has recently shed 440 managers.[139] In the larger areas of desert urbanization, the mood has changed dramatically. In 2006, construction noise echoed across the valley and construction dust filled the skies. In 2007, new home sales decreased by almost 46% and many construction sites are now quiet with bulldozers parked and construction crews gone.[140] The principal developer of Lake Las Vegas failed to meet 500 million dollars in payments and ownership passed to an investment consortium led by Credit Suisse.[141] Coyote Springs has postponed its grand opening spectacular. The newest image of the city is one of foreclosure signs and "foreclosure bus tours" are taking those with extra cash on the rounds of distressed property sales: the valley has 7000 foreclosed homes.[142] February 2008 saw more foreclosures than combined new and existing home sales.[143] In many aspects, Las Vegas now reflects a tale of two cities. Always focused on the new, Las Vegas may have finally been caught by its own history.

We learned from our journeys through the Las Vegas Valley and the Mojave Desert that these sites of transition offer far too many perspectives and insights to serve as a single model of urbanization or to fit into categories of praise or dismissal. Las Vegas developed from a western desert oasis to the "American" city of Venturi and Scott Brown, evolving further through expansion fueled in part by north-south migration before becoming the global city it is today. Returning from our tours through the real, reel and read topographies as a modernist counter-site of a sublime otherworldliness, a postmodern pastiche of an all-American everyday, and as a postcolonialist hybrid landscape shaped by processes of extraction, abstraction, militarization and recreation, questions of the successes and failures of urbanization in an extreme and fragile environment are of urgent concern. Important answers lie in imagining, imaging, and interpreting these complex and dynamic sites of transition.

1   Margaretta Lovell, "Picturing 'A City for a Summer': Paintings of the World's Columbian Exposition" in: *The Art Bulletin*, 78:1, (1996): 40–55.

2   For Frederick Jackson Turner's thesis, see his *The Frontier in American History*, (New York: Holt, 1920) or the many reprint editions.

3   Arnold Knightly, "Plaza Project Gets First OK. Planning Panel Gives Nod to Project; County Commission up Next" in: *Las Vegas Review-Journal*, (12/20/07): D1.

4   Articles addressing Las Vegas had appeared prior to the publication of the original over-size book *Learning from Las Vegas* (1972). See: Robert Venturi and Denise Scott Brown, "A Significance for A&P Parking Lots or Learning from Las Vegas" in: *Architectural Forum*, 128:2, (March 1968): 36–43.

5   Reyner Banham, *Scenes in America Deserta*, (Salt Lake City, UT: Gibbs M. Smith, 1982): 16.

6   Ibid.: 17.

7   Ibid.: 224.

8   John Beck, "Without Form and Void. The American Desert as Trope and Terrain" in: *Nepantla: Views from South*, 2:1, (2001): 63–83; 75.

9   Reyner Banham, See note 5: 86–87.

10 Donald Appleyard, Kevin Lynch and John Myer, *The View from the Road*, (Cambridge, MA: MIT Press, 1964): Preface.

11 Ibid.: 63.

12 Ibid.: 4. Additionally, the "kinesthetic sensations are like those of the dance or the amusement park."

13 Ibid.: 47.

14 Fred Koetter, "On Robert Venturi, Denise Scott Brown and Steven Izenour's Learning from Las Vegas" in: *Oppositions* 3, (1974): 100.

15 Reyner Banham, *Los Angeles. The Architecture of Four Ecologies*, (Berkeley: University of California Press, 2001): 5.

16 Reyner Banham, See note 5: 17.

17 Alessandra Ponte and Marisa Trubiano, "The House of Light and Entropy: Inhabiting the American Desert" in: *Assemblage*, 30, (1996): 12–31; 23, 17.

18 John C. Van Dyke, *The Desert. Further Studies in Natural Appearances*, (New York: Charles Scribner's Sons, 1906): 25–26.

19 Reyner Banham, See note 5: 61–62.

20 William Fox, *In the Desert of Desire. Las Vegas and the Culture of Spectacle*, (Reno, NV: University of Nevada Press, 2005): xi.

21 David Wrobel, "Beyond the Frontier-Region Dichotomy" in: *The Pacific Historical Review*, 65:3, (1996): 401–429; 401.

22 John Beck, See note 8: 64.

23 John Beck, See note 8: 65.

24 Helen Carlson, "Mine Names on the Nevada Comstock Lode" in: *Western Folklore*, 15:1, (1956): 49–57; 49.

25 Quoted in David Johnson, "Industry and the Individual on the Far Western Frontier: A Case Study of Political and Social Change in Early Nevada" in: *The Pacific Historical Review*, 51:3, (1982): 243–64; 246.

26 Eugene Moehring, "The Comstock Urban Network" in: *The Pacific Historical Review*, 66:3, (1997): 337–62; 341.

27 Ibid.: 343.

28 Ronald James, Richard Adkins, Rachel Hartigan, "Competition and Coexistence in the Laundry: A View of the Comstock" in: *The Western Historical Quarterly*, 25:5, (1994): 164–84.

29 Eugene Moehring, See note 26: 348–49.

30 Eugene Moehring, See note 26: 353.

31 Scott Fields, "The Earth's Open Wounds. Abandoned and Orphaned Mines" in: *Environmental Health Perspectives*, 111:3, (2003): A154–A161; A159.

32 Associated Press, "Abandoned Mines luring the Curious to Injury, Sudden Death" in: *Las Vegas Review-Journal*, (09/04/96): 4B.

33 J. Davitt McAteer, "Abandoned Mines a Real Danger in West" in: *Las Vegas Review-Journal*, (01/18/00): 7B.

34 Lawrence Mower, "Deadly Pitfalls Waiting Off-Road. Bikers, ATV Riders Risk Falling into Thousands of Nevada Shafts" in: *Las Vegas Review-Journal*, (09/09/07): B1.

35 Stephanie Mrozek et al., "Decorative Landscaping Rock as a Source for Heavy Metal Contamination, Las Vegas, Nevada" in: *Soil and Sediment Contamination*, 15:5, (2006): 471–80; 478–79. See Gian Galassi, "Some Decorative Landscaping Rock Could Pose Environmental, Human Health Risk" in: *UNLV News Release*, (06/09/06) http://publicaffairs.unlv.edu/news-MediaCenter.html?id=338 (accessed 12/30/07).

36 Adrienne Packer, "Bonnie Springs Ranch Homes OK'd" in: *Las Vegas Review-Journal*, (07/22/05): 4B.

37 Edward Burtynsky, *Quarries*, (Göttingen: Steidl, 2007).

38 Richard Misrach, *Desert Cantos*, (Albuquerque, NM: Uni. of New Mexico Press, 1987

49 Richard Misrach, quoted in: Anne Wilkes Tucker, "A Problem of Beauty" in: A.W. Tucker with R. Solnit, *Crimes and Splendor: The Desert Cantos of Richard Misrach*, (Houston, TX: The Museum of Fine Arts, 1996): 16.

50 Ibid.: 16.

51 Ibid.: 15.

52 Richard Misrach with Miriam Wysang Misrach, *Bravo 20: The Bombing of the American West*, (Baltimore: Johns Hopkins University Press, 1990); Richard Misrach, *Violent Legacies: Three Cantos*, (New York: Aperture, 1992).

53 Keith Rogers, "Reid Seeks Probe in Horse Deaths. Nitrate Poisoning near Nellis Test Range Cited" in: *Las Vegas Review-Journal*, (08/25/07): B2.

54 Keith Rogers, "61 Horses Died in '88 at Test Site" in: *Las Vegas Review-Journal*, (11/24/07): B1.

55 Valerie Kuletz, *The Tainted Desert: Environmental and Social Ruin in the American West*, (New York: Routledge, 1998): 40.

56 Rebecca Solnit, *Savage Dreams: A Journey into the Landscape Wars of the American West*, (Berkeley: University of California, 2000): 5. (original printing by Sierra Club Books, 1994).

57 Tom Vanderbilt, *Survival City: Adventures among the Ruins of Atomic America*, (New York: Princeton Architectural Press, 2002): 92.

58 "Area Stands up Well" in: *New York Times*, (05/06/55): 12.

59 "Final Nevada Test of '55 Uses Supersonic Jets for the First Time" in: *New York Times*, (05/16/55): 1.

50 Message from the Test Manager of the Joint Test Organization, Camp Mercury Nevada (February, 1955). www.fourmilab.ch/etexts/www/atomic_tests_nevada/ (accessed 12/30/07).

1 Ken Cooper, "'Zero Pays the House': The Las Vegas Novel and Atomic Roulette" in: *Contemporary Literature*, 33:3, (1992): 528–544; 530.

2 Michael Broadhead, "Notes on the Military Presence in Nevada: 1843–1988" in: *Nevada Historical Society Quarterly*, 32:4, (1989). Quoted in David Loomis, *Combat Zoning: Military Land-Use Planning in Nevada*, (Reno, NV: University of Nevada Press, 1993): 10.

3 David Loomis, *Combat Zoning: Military Land-Use Planning in Nevada*, (Reno, NV: University of Nevada Press, 1993): vii.

4 Harold Parker, "Good Roads Movement" in: *Annals of the American Academy of Political and Social Science*, 40, (1912): 51–57; 53.

55 Peter Hugill, "Good Roads and the Automobile in the United States 1880–1929" in: *Geographical Review*, 72:3, (1982): 327–49; 328.

56 Frederic Paxson, "The Highway Movement, 1916–1935" in: *The American Historical Review*, 51:2, (1946): 236–53; 238.

57 Marguerite Shaffer, "'See America First': Re-Envisioning Nation and Region through Western Tourism" in: *The Pacific Historical Review*, 65:4, (1996): 559–581; 559, 564–65. See also: M. Shaffer, *See America First. Tourism and National Identity 1880–1940*, (Washington, DC: Smithsonian, 2001).

58 Peter Hugill, "Good Roads and the Automobile in the United States 1880–1929" in: *Geographical Review*, 72:3, (1982): 327–349; 338.

59 Frederic Paxson, "The Highway Movement, 1916–1935" in: *The American Historical Review*, 51:2 (1946): 236–53; 243, 245.

60 Kerwin Klein, "Frontier Products: Tourism, Consumerism, and the Southwestern Public Lands, 1890–1990" in: *The Pacific Historical Review*, 62:1, (1993): 39–71; 57.

61 Vernon Metcalf, secretary of the Nevada Land and Livestock Association (1921). Quoted in Thomas Cox, "Before the Casino: James G. Scrugham, State Parks, and Nevada's Quest for Tourism" in: *The Western Historical Quarterly*, 24:3, (1993): 332–350; 337.

62 Robert Glendinning, "Desert Change: A Study of the Boulder Dam Area" in: *The Scientific Monthly*, 61:3, (1945): 181–193; 193. This article emphasized the importance of the Boulder Dam in attracting tourists. Despite the war, by 1945 Boulder Dam had already attracted some five million visitors.

63 Public Law 88-577, 88th Congress, Session 4, September 3, 1964.

64 "The Fragile Desert" in: *Science News*, 110:2, (1976): 24.

65 Felicity Barringer and William Yardley, "Public Lands: Surge in Off-Roading Stirs Dust and Debate in West" in: *New York Times*, (12/30/07). Front Page.

66 www.rrpartners.com/work/case_study.cfm?xclient=118 (accessed 12/30/07).

67 Quoted in Patricia Limerick, "The Shadows of Heaven Itself" in: J. Robb and W. Riebsame (eds.), *Atlas of the New West: Portrait of a Changing Region*, (New York: Norton, 1997): 151–179; 177–78.

68 Kerwin Klein, See note 60: 43.

69 Kerwin Klein, See note 60: 43–44.

70 Kerwin Klein, See note 60: 50.

71 Edward Buscombe, "Inventing Monument Valley: Nineteenth-Century Landscape Photography and the Western Film" in: J. Kitses and G. Rickman, *The Western Reader*, (New York: Limelight, 1998): 115–130.

72 *Mad Max 2: The Road Warrior* (George Miller, 1981), *Easy Rider* (Dennis Hopper, 1969), *Vanishing Point* (Richard Sarafian, 1971), *Thelma & Louise* (Ridley Scott, 1991).

73 See Mark Klett et al., *Second View: The Rephotographic Survey Project*, (Albuquerque, NM: University of New Mexico Press, 1990), *Third Views, Second Sights: A Rephotographic Survey of the American West*, (Albuquerque, NM: Museum of New Mexico Press, 2004), and *After the Ruins, 1906 and 2006: Rephotographing the San Francisco Earthquake and Fire*, (Berkeley: University of California Press, 2006).

74 Frederick Jackson Turner, "The Colonization of the West" in *The American Historical Review*, 11:2, (1906): 303, and Frederick Jackson Turner, *The Frontier in American History*, (New York, 1920): 1.

75 Patricia Limerick, "The Trail to Santa Fe: The Unleashing of the Western Public Intellectual" in: P. Limerick, C.A. Milner II, and C.E. Rankin (eds.), *Trails: Toward a New Western History*, (Lawrence, KS: University of Kansas Press, 1991): 69.

76 Ibid.: 69–70.

77 David Wrobel, "What on Earth Has Happened to the New Western History?" in: *The Historian*, 66:3, (2004): 437–441.

78 David Wrobel, "Beyond the Frontier-Region Dichotomy" in: *Pacific Historical Review*, 65:3, (1996): 401–429; 426.

79 Richard White, "From Wilderness to Hybrid Landscapes: The Cultural Turn in Environmental History" in: *The Historian*, 66:3, (2004): 557–564; 558.

80 Patricia Limerick, "Going West and Ending Up Global" in: *The Western Historical Quarterly*, 32:1 (2001): 5.

81 Eugene Moehring, *Resort City in the Sunbelt: Las Vegas, 1930–1970*, (Reno: University of Nevada Press, 1989).

82 Hal Rothman, *Neon Metropolis. How Las Vegas Started the Twenty-First Century*, (New York: Routledge, 2002): 63–88.

83 Patricia Ventura, "Learning From Globalization-Era Las Vegas" in: *Southern Quarterly*, 42:1, (2003): 97–112; 98.

84 Ibid.: 110.

85 Robert Venturi and Denise Scott Brown, "A Significance for A&P Parking Lots or Learning from Las Vegas" in: *Architectural Forum*, 128:2, (1968): 36–43, 89, 91; 39.

86 David Schwartz, *Suburban Xanadu: The Casino Resort on the Las Vegas Strip and Beyond*, (New York: Routledge, 2003): 16.

87 Ibid.: 33.

88 William Eadington, "The Casino Gaming Industry: A Study of Political Economy" in: *Annals of the American Academy of Political and Social Science*, 474, (1984): 23–35; 24, 32, 24.

89 David Schwartz, See note 86: 8.

90 Norman Klein, "Scripting Las Vegas: Noir Naifs, Junking Up, and the New Strip" in: H. Rothman and M. Davis (eds.), *The Grit Beneath the Glitter: Tales from the Real Las Vegas*, (Berkeley: University of California Press, 2002): 21.

91 Ellen Nakashima, "From Casinos to Counterterrorism. Las Vegas Surveillance, U.S. Security Efforts Involve Similar Tactics" in: *The Washington Post*, (10/22/07): A01. The song is by the British rock band *The Who*.

92 Ibid.: A01.

93 Charles Bock, *Beautiful Children*, (New York: Random House, 2008): 183.

94 Alan Hess, *Viva Las Vegas: After-Hours Architecture*; foreword by Robert Venturi, Denise Scott Brown, Steven Izenour, (San Francisco: Chronicle Books, 1993): 8.

95 Mark Gottdiener, Claudia Collins, and David Dickens, *Las Vegas: the Social Production of an All-American City*, (Malden, MA: Blackwell, 1999): xiii.

96 Michael Dear, "Imagining Postmodern Urbanism" in: M. Dear (ed.), *From Chicago to L.A.: Making Sense of Urban Theory*, (Thousand Oaks, CA: Sage, 2002): 85–92; 91.

97 Hal Rothman, See note 82: xxvi.

98 Hal Rothman, See note 82: xxvii.

99 Howard Stutz, "Strip vs. Strip" in: *Las Vegas Review-Journal*, (10/24/07): D1.

100 Associated Press, "Venetian Macau said to draw 114,000 visitors in first 24 hours" in: *Las Vegas Review-Journal*, (09/06/07). www.lvrj.com/business/9612252.html (accessed 12/30/07).

101 David Barboza, "It's a Brawl. China's Gamblers Are the Prize" in: *The New York Times*, (03/25/07): 3.1.

102 Gary Rivlin, "Newcomer to Casinos Counts on Knowing the Players" in: *The New York Times*, (12/29/07): C2.

103 Graham Kelly, "Spain Deals 007 in for new Las Vegas" in: *The Sunday Times*, (11/25/07). www.timesonline.co.uk/tol/news/world/europe/article2936817.ec (accessed 12/30/07).

104 Eugene Moehring, "The Civil War and Town Founding in the Intermountain West" in: *The Western Historical Quarterly*, 28:3, (1997): 316–341; 319.

105 Barbara Murray, "MGM, Dubai World Close JV for $7B CityCenter Project in Las Vegas" in: *Commercial Property News*, (11/16/07).

106 www.citycenter.com (accessed 01/05/08).

107 Anon. Editorial, "Auctioning Federal Real Estate. Is Las Vegas Running Out of Private Land?" in: *Las Vegas Review-Journal,* (10/08/07): B8.

108 Brian Wargo, "Hillside Development Boasts Dramatic Views" in: *Business Las Vegas,* 01/26/07–02/01/07. www.inbusinesslasvegas.com/2007/01/26/feature3.html (accessed 12/30/07).

109 Henry Brean, "Henderson Explosions: Blasts Irritate Homeowners" in: *Las Vegas Review-Journal,* (03/21/05): 1B.

110 Buck Wargo, "Sink or Swim. Lake Las Vegas Must Sell Land to Stay Afloat" in: *Business in Las Vegas,* 11/16/07–11/22/07.

111 Michael Dear, *The Postmodern Urban Condition,* (Oxford: Blackwell, 2000): 206.

112 Norman Klein, See note 90: 19.

113 Norman Klein, See note 90: 21.

114 Marc Reisner, *Cadillac Desert: The American West and its Disappearing Water,* (New York: Penguin, 1986, 1993): 14.

115 Tim Barnett and David Pierce, "When will Lake Mead go Dry?" in: *Water Resources Research,* 44, (2008).

116 *Estates West,* (Winter, 2007): 40.

117 Steve Tetreault, "Judge lets Lawsuit against Coyote Springs Proceed" in: *Las Vegas Review-Journal,* (09/27/07): B4.

118 Nate Berg, "Growth Keeps Las Vegas Water Chief Busy" in: *Planetizen: Urban Planning, Design and Development Network,* www.planetizen.com.

119 Bettina Boxall and Ashley Powers, "Colorado River Water Deal is Reached; The Interior Secretary Calls it an 'Agreement to Share Adversity'" in: *Los Angeles Times,* (12/14/07): A14.

120 James Deacon, Austin Williams, Cindy Deacon Williams, and Jack Williams, "Fueling Population Growth in Las Vegas: How Large-Scale Groundwater Withdrawal Could Burn Regional Biodiversity" in: *BioScience,* 57:8, (2007): 688–98; 688.

121 Ibid.: 688.

122 Bettina Boxall, "Sin City Covets Thy Aquifers; Vegas' Drinking Problem is Nevada Ranchers' Headache" in: *Los Angeles Times,* (03/07/07): A1.

123 Kerwin Klein, See note 60: 43.

124 Ackbar Abbas, "Exotic with an 'X'" in: J. Ockman and S. Frausto (eds.), *Architourism Authentic, Escapist, Exotic, Spectacular,* (Munich: Prestel, 2005): 105.

125 Ibid.: 105.

126 Mark Hostetler, "Live and Play in Coyote Springs": www.articlesbase.com/real-estate-articles/live-and-play-in-coyote-springs-265489.html, Posted: 22-11-2007.

127 Coyote Springs, Landscapes, Spring 2006, p. 5. www.coyotesprings.com/press/newsletter_spring_2006.pdf (accessed 12/30/07).

128 PGA Announces Western PGA Village, Site Set for Southern Nevada, www.coyotesprings.com/press/045953%20RR-1.pdf (accessed 12/30/07).

129 www.coyotesprings.com/golf_pga.html (accessed 12/30/07).

130 Ackbar Abbas, See note 124: 106.

131 Ackbar Abbas, *Hong Kong: Culture and the Politics of Disappearance,* (Minneapolis: University of Minnesota Press): 48.

132 Ibid.: 48.

133 Hal Rothman, "Shedding Skin and Shifting Shape: Tourism in the Modern West" in: D. Wrobel and P. Long (eds.), *Seeing and Being Seen: Tourism in the American West,* (Lawrence, KS, University of Kansas Press, 2001): 100–120; 102.

134 Hal Rothman and Mike Davis, "Introduction: The Many Faces of Las Vegas" in: H. Rothman and M. Davis (eds.), *The Grit Beneath the Glitter: Tales from the Real Las Vegas,* (Berkeley: University of California Press, 2002): 1.

135 Hal Rothman, See note 133: 103.

136 Hal Rothman, See note 133: 103.

137 Norman Klein, See note 90: 17, 27.

138 Benjamin Spillman, "LV Visitor Count Rises to 39.2 Million People in 2007" in: *Las Vegas Review-Journal,* (02/13/08): D1.

139 Howard Stutz, "Share Prices for Major Casino Companies Drop" in: *Las Vegas Review-Journal,* (04/16/08): D1.

140 Hubble Smith, "Home Sales Tumble in 2007" in: *Las Vegas Review-Journal,* (01/22/08): D1.

141 Arnold M. Knightly, "Lake Las Vegas Properties Change Hands" in: *Las Vegas Review-Journal,* (01/09/08): D1.

142 Jennifer Robison, "Home Sellers Warp Time" in: *Las Vegas Review-Journal,* (02/16/08): A1.

143 Hubble Smith, "Home Market Keeps Slipping" in: *Las Vegas Review-Journal,* (03/19/08): D1.

Kehrseiten & Ränder

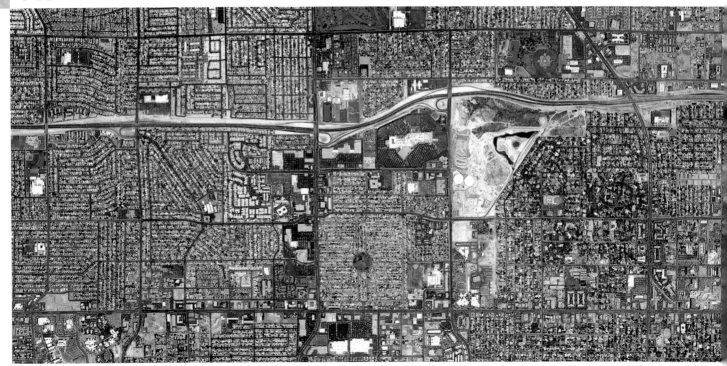

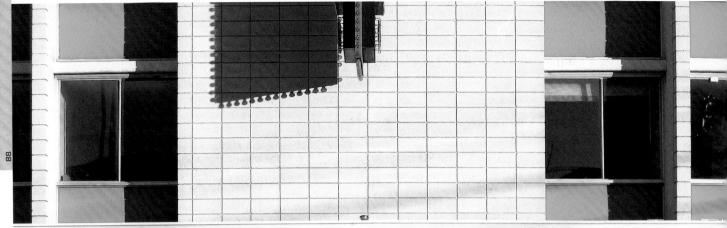

Zeichen & Spuren

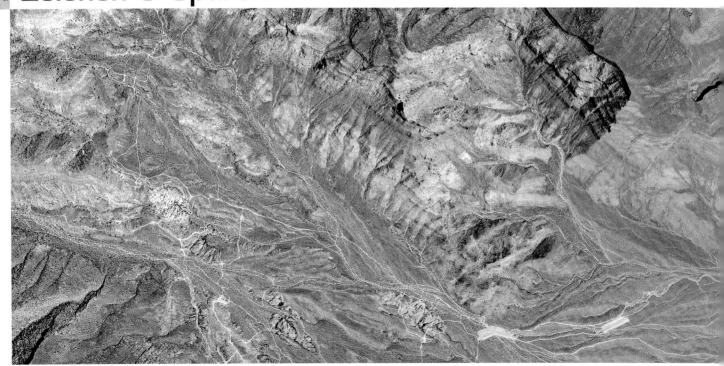

BLUE
MAN
GROUP
"A SENSATION!"
—TIME MAGAZINE
THE
VENETIAN®
82
LAMAR

Mobilität & Stabilität

Mobility & Stability

FIESTA
COMING SOON!
-New Parking Garage
-New Race & Sports Book
-More Of Your Favorite Slots
RIGHT LANE ENDS
MEGATRUX
TRANSPORTATION. INC.

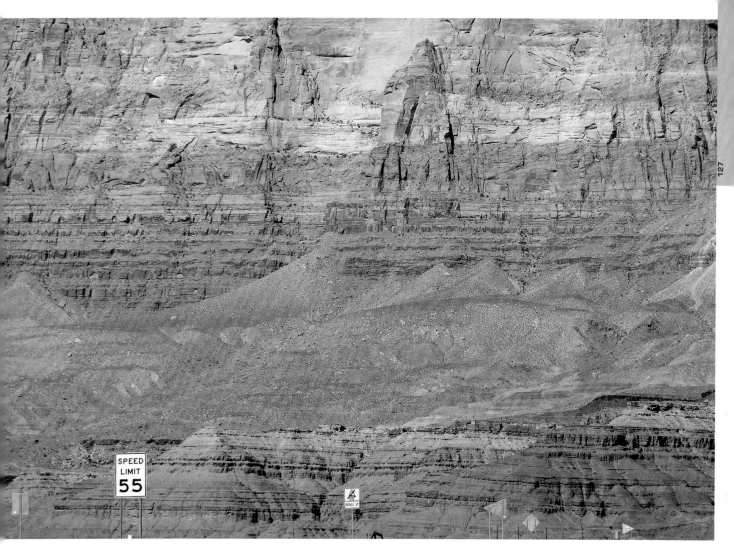

Versorgen & Entsorgen

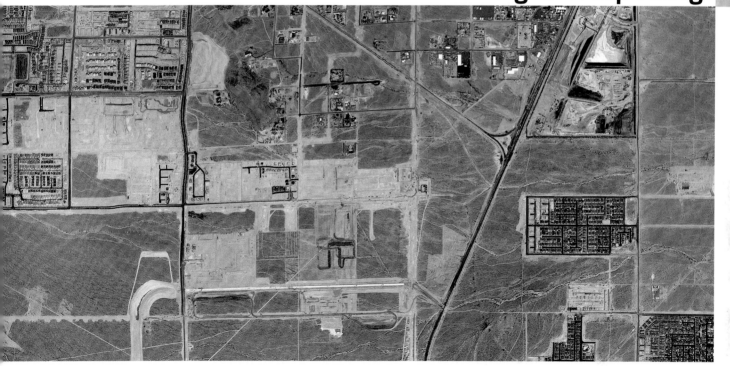

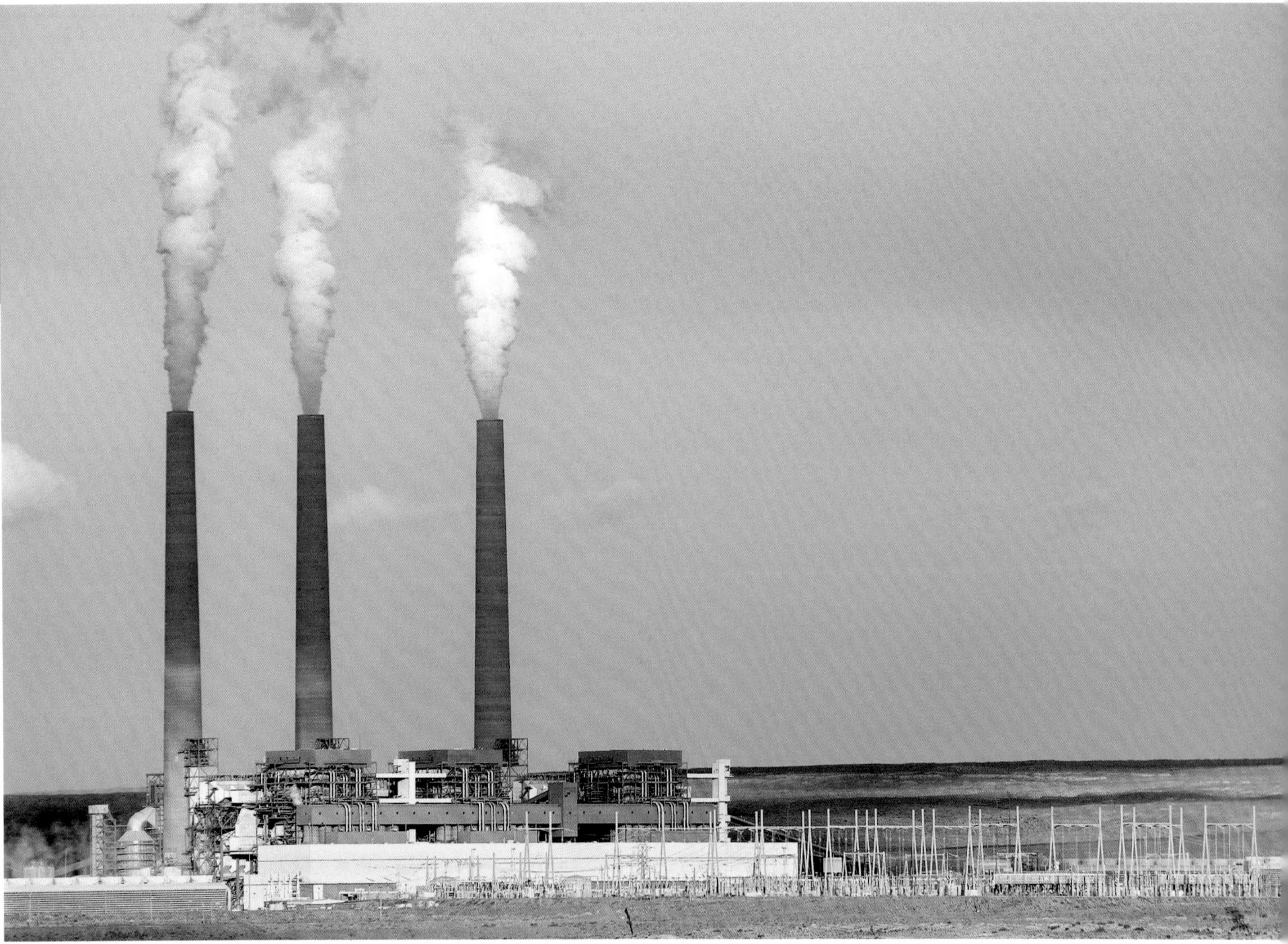

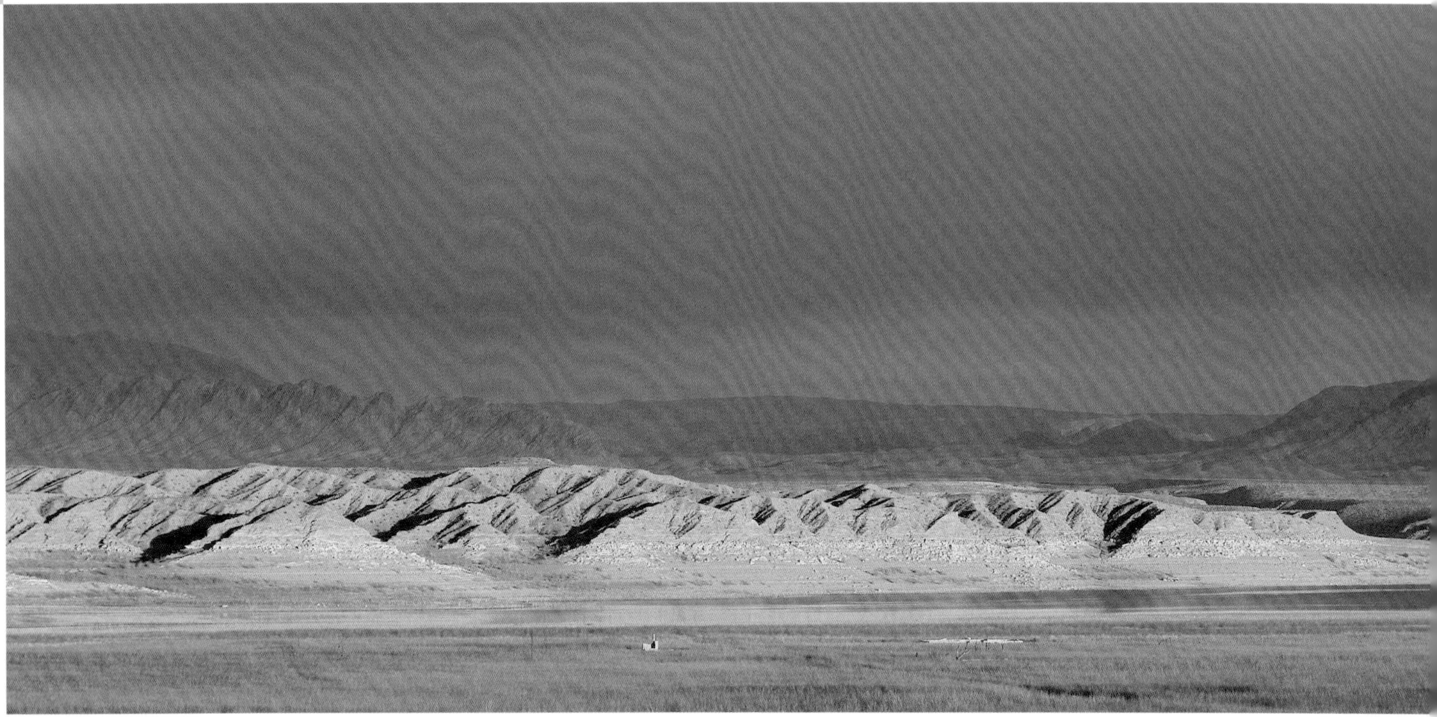

Abstraktion & Extraktion

152

CANYON EDGE HOMES
216.4663
LUXURY HOMES OF LAS VEGAS
CALL TODAY
702 216-4663
SECURITY

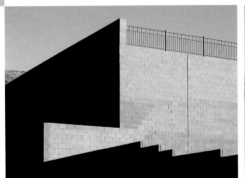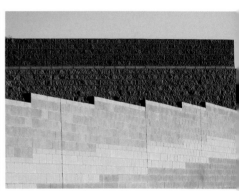

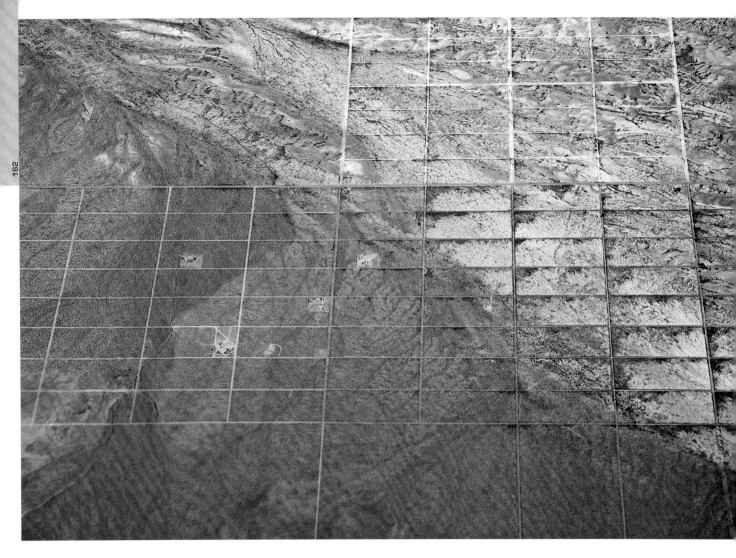

Abschaben & Ausbreiten

Nachwort

Die gezeigten Bilder projizieren weder Ideale städtischer Entwicklung noch lösen sie soziale oder umweltbezogene Probleme. Vielmehr bieten sie eine dritte Sichtweise, die die Verbindungen zwischen den Räumen alltäglicher Produktion und Konsumption, der Schaffung physischer und virtueller Orte sowie lokaler und globaler Investition aufzeigt. Ortsansässige kommentierten diese Bilder mit „ich sehe dies jeden Tag, habe es jedoch nie wirklich ‚gesehen'". Der klassischen architektonischen Trope des „Sehenlernens" entsprechend und durch die Kommentare ermutigt, lernten wir, die Wüstenstadt jenseits der blendenden Lichter des Strip zu sehen.

Die Urbanisierung der Mojave-Wüste: Las Vegas zeigt eine hybride Landschaft, die durch Urbanisierungspraktiken ge- und überformt wird. Diese Praktiken schließen die Topografien der Ein- und Ausgrenzung (*Kehrseiten & Ränder*) ein, wo eingedämmte Orte natürlichen Ressourcen (S. 74) und segregierte Umwelt (S. 75) „exklusiven" Kasinos (S. 90, 92) gegenüberstehen. Diese Exklusivität verbirgt die Außenseiterrolle, die sozialen Randgruppen zugewiesen wird. Die Praktiken beinhalten weiterhin die De- und Reterritorialisierungen (*Zeichen & Spuren*), die durch die Mischung physischer und virtueller Räume die Wüste mit den imaginären Reichen des Spektakulären (S. 96, 106, 107), des Begehrens (S. 97, 105), der Macht (S. 99, 103) und des Außergewöhnlichen (S. 100–102) verbinden. Sie beleuchten Konversionen zwischen Nutzungs- und Wirtschaftsmodellen (*Mobilität & Stabilität*) und verbinden so eine transitorische Arbeiterschaft (S. 113–15, 120, 121) mit dem Verbrauch von Ressourcen und Waren (S. 112, 116–19, 122–27). Darüber hinaus verbinden sie lokale und regionale Maßstäbe (*Versorgen & Entsorgen*) durch Infrastrukturen der Energieversorgung (S. 130, 131, 133–35) und Topografien der Abfall- (S. 137, 145) und Wasserwirtschaft (S. 132, 138–40, 142–44). Zugleich fusionieren sie industrielle und postindustrielle Nutzungen (*Abstraktion & Extraktion*) mit ihren eingeebneten Geografien (S. 150–61) und eingeschriebenen Geometrien (S. 162, 163). Zuletzt zeigen sie Praktiken der Überlagerung (*Abschaben & Ausbreiten*), die zugleich Landschaften industrialisierten Begehrens, exotischen Dekors und umweltbezogener Schäden schichten und die Nähe der Topografien des Ab- und Aufbaus (S. 167, 184), des Wasserbaus (S. 178, 185, 186) sowie Import-Landschaften (S. 170–75, 185, 187–89) und -Typologien offenlegen, die von italienischen Villen zu „kosmopolitanen" Blockstrukturen reichen.

Somit fokussiert *Die Urbanisierung der Mojave Wüste: Las Vegas* die nahtlosen Oberflächen drapierter Neonlichter, Vorhangfassaden und Landschaftszüge und enthüllt die Schichten, die die sozialen, kulturellen, und umweltbezogenen Implikationen der Urbanisierung einer zugleich rauhen und fragilen Wüste aufzeigen.

Epilogue

The images presented above do not project ideals of urban development or solve social and environmental problems. Rather, the images offer a "third sight" that makes visible the complex interstitial spaces of everyday production and consumption tied to physical and virtual place making as well as local and global investment. Locals have responded to these images with comments such as "I see these things everyday, but have never really 'seen' them before". It is a classic architectural trope to "learn to see" and, heartened by such responses, we have learned to see a desert city beyond the blinding lights of the Las Vegas Strip.

Urbanizing the Mojave Desert: Las Vegas presents a profoundly complex environment, a hybrid landscape shaped and reshaped by practices of everyday urbanization. Such practices include the fragmented topographies of in- and exclusion (*rears & edges*) where confined sites of natural resources (p. 74) and segregated environments (p. 75) are mirrored by "exclusive" casinos (pp. 90, 92). In turn, such spectacular exclusivity conceals the peripheral role assigned various economic and social groups. These practices also include the de- and reterritorialization (*signs & traces*) associated with blending physical and virtual spaces that connect the desert landscape to imaginary realms of the spectacular (pp. 96, 106, 107), desire (pp. 97, 105), power (pp. 99, 103), the exceptional (pp. 100–102), and the promised

(pp. 108, 109). They illuminate conversions between land use and economics (*mobility & stability*), linking a transitory work force (pp. 113–15, 120, 121) with the consumption of resources and commodities (pp. 112, 116–19, 122–27). They also network local and regional scales (*providing & disposing*) through infrastructures of energy production (pp. 130, 131, 133–35) and the topographies of waste- (pp. 137, 145) and water-management (pp.132, 138–40, 142–44). These practices fuse industrial and postindustrial activities (*abstraction & extraction*) with their leveled geographies (pp.150–61) and inscribed geometries (pp. 162, 163). Finally, these are the practices of imbrication (*scraping & sprawling*), overlapping landscapes of industrialized desire, exotic decorum, and environmental damage; exposing the proximity of topographies of extraction and construction (pp. 167, 184), the artificiality of water diversions and catchments (pp. 178, 185, 186), imported landscapes (pp. 170–75, 185, 187–89), and constructions ranging from Italian villas to "cosmopolitan" blocks.

As such, *Urbanizing the Mojave Desert: Las Vegas* reframes the seamless surfaces of draped neon lights, curtain walls, and landscape features layered onto the Mojave's stark topography, uncovering distinct strata that respatialize the social, cultural, and environmental implications of urbanizing a fierce yet fragile desert.

Bildnachweise & Kooperationspartner
Image Credits & Cooperating Partner

John C. Dohrenwend, Southwest Satellite Imaging: S./p. 8.

Special Collections, University of Nevada Las Vegas Libraries: S./pp. 14, 19, 31, 38, 39.

Southern Nevada Water Authority: S./p. 63.

Landiscor Aerial Information: S./pp. 15, 72, 73, 94, 95, 110, 111, 128, 129, 146, 147.

Die Autoren: Alle weiteren Abbildungen. Diese zeigen das Las Vegas Valley und fogende Orte:/All other images courtesy of the authors. These are of the Las Vegas Valley and the following locations: Coyote Springs, NV: dust jacket and page 189; Crystal Springs, NV: S./p. 102; Boulder City, NV: S./p. 168; Lake Mead, NV: S./pp. 74, 124, 132, 142 [oben und unten links/upper and lower left, oben rechts/upper right]; Lake Mead at St. Thomas, NV: S./p. 144; Overton, NV: S./p. 125; Blue Diamond, NV: S./p. 152 [Mitte rechts/right middle]; Sloan, NV: S./p. 151, 152 [Mitte links/left middle]; Sandy Valley, NV: S./p. 122; Old Spanish Trail Highway near Pahrump, NV: S./p. 162; Silver Peak near Goldfield, NV: S./p. 163; Lake Powell, AZ: S./pp. 142 [Mitte oben/upper middle, unten rechts/lower right], 143; Paige, AZ: S./p. 130; Lee's Ferry, AZ: S./pp: 126, 127; Nothing, AZ: S./pp. 119, 123; Palm Springs, CA: S./p. 138 [oben links/upper left]; Death Valley, CA: S./p. 138 [unten rechts/lower right].

This project is partly funded by a grant from the Nevada Arts Council, a division of the Department of Cultural Affairs, and the National Endowment for the Arts, a federal agency.

In undertaking *Urbanizing the Mojave Desert: Las Vegas*, the authors linked the concerns of Las Vegas and the Mojave Desert to other desert cities and regions. As a close neighbor, Phoenix, Arizona was a logical choice and the Phoenix Urban Research Laboratory (PURL) has been an exceptional cooperating partner in issues pertaining to urban growth, sustainable urban environments, as well as the preservation of natural environments and resources. We therefore include the following statement from PURL:

"The Phoenix Urban Research Laboratory is an extension – part think tank, part design center – of the College of Design at Arizona State University. Our mission is to inspire creative thinking and concrete action that will empower the transformation of the postwar city of the twentieth century into the sustainable metropolis of the twenty-first century. While our focus – our laboratory – is metropolitan Phoenix, our purview is wide-ranging. Indeed, Phoenix is now grappling with the critical questions that confront cities around the globe: how can we adapt the low-density, automobile-centric urban environments we have been building for half a century? What new development patterns, what new planning models, will allow our late twentieth century cities to mature successfully, to achieve true environmental, economic, and social resilience?"